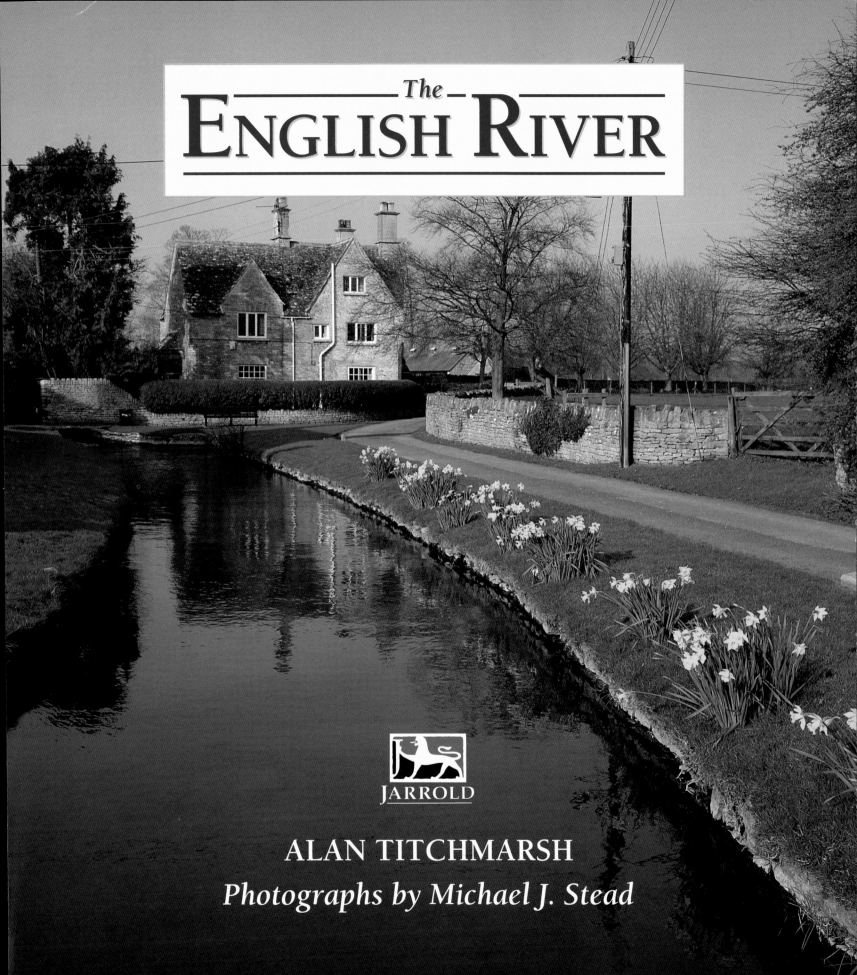

The ENGLISH RIVER

JARROLD

ALAN TITCHMARSH

Photographs by Michael J. Stead

Acknowledgements

So many people have helped me with this book. My thanks go to Jan Tavinor for her research and to the NRA for supplying much useful information and data, to Michael Stead for his brilliant photographs and candid remarks, to Anne Priestley for her good-humoured editing and to Kim Smith for the sensitive design. Thanks also to Ian McIntyre for asking me to write the book in the first place. My family have cheerfully helped me trace some of the rivers (not always easy), and Ordnance Survey maps have become a passion.
To everyone who has patiently answered the questions of a bewildered man with a crumpled map in his hands, I offer my grateful thanks. Any mistakes are my own. A.T.

The Publishers would like to thank the following for permission to use their photographs:
ARC Wildfowl Centre p. 48 (top); The John Lewis Partnership p. 94; The Otter Trust,
Earsham p. 66 (top left); Pensthorpe Waterfowl Trust/Geoff du Feu p. 58 (top).

The photographs on pp. 57 (right), 65 (bottom), 68 (top), 84 (bottom left), 104 (bottom),
112 (top) and 149 (top right) were supplied by Jarrold Publishing.

THE ENGLISH RIVER

Designed and produced by Parke Sutton Publishing Limited, Norwich
for Jarrold Publishing, Norwich

Text copyright © 1993 Alan Titchmarsh
Photographs copyright © 1993 Michael J. Stead (except those listed above)
This edition copyright © 1993 Jarrold Publishing
ISBN 0-7117-0644-1

Edited by Anne Priestley
Designed by Kim Smith

Printed in Belgium

Contents

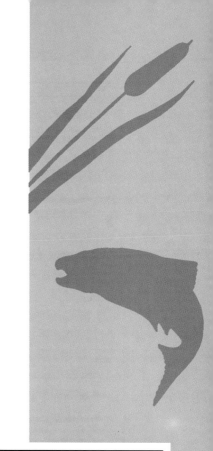

To my friends
on the river bank:
Suzanne and Andy,
Steve and Marion,
Richard and Mandy
and Bob.

Introduction

I cannot tell you when I first fell under the spell of the river bank. It was long before Moley and Ratty came into my consciousness when *The Wind in the Willows* was read out loud at school. Before I could crawl I was taken for picnics on the pebble-strewn banks of the River Wharfe in Yorkshire, and I continued to be taken there throughout my childhood, to catch minnows, to skim smooth, flat stones across the water to the opposite bank, and to paddle into the amber depths with trousers rolled up high.

From then on rivers became associated with relaxation and freedom. To boat on the Thames, to fish in a chalk stream or simply to watch dippers bob in the brisk water of a rippling beck still gives me deep and lasting pleasure. To be asked to write a book about such delights came as an agreeable surprise.

But what sort of book is it? It is not a guidebook. Even less is it a scientific survey dealing with the management of natural water courses. True enough, it examines each of eighteen rivers from source to estuary or to the point at which a river becomes part of a larger one, but it is also subject to my whims and fancies.

Those who live on the Tyne, Tees or Wear, the Yare, the Wensum or the Waveney may feel short-changed because less space is devoted to them as individuals. My excuse is that they are close to one another and so treated as a trio. The Medway also is treated as a tributary of the Thames, which it is not, and I apologise to it and the Kentish Men and Men of Kent for the insult.

What I hope this book does do is to give you a feel of the different characters of the rivers. I also hope it persuades you to go and have a look at them. It is a celebration of the English river but also a frank look at the way in which we have sometimes abused our waterways. By the mid-seventies some rivers were little more than open sewers. Over the last twenty years much has been done by water authorities and by the National Rivers Authority to treat sewage effluent before it is expelled into rivers and to reduce pollution. But can a quango such as the NRA be both guardian of a river and promoter of its resources? Only, I suspect, with difficulty.

The abstraction of water has resulted in many rivers being bled dry. The transportation of water from one river to another to maintain flows affects nutrient content, temperature and water level, often with harmful effects on river life. Rivers are fragile ecological systems, a fact which has become only too apparent in recent years.

Some may think that in succeeding chapters I've let off the polluters and abstractors lightly. That is not my intention, but I see little point in repeatedly venting my spleen throughout a book which is determined to champion the English river rather than bemoan its fate.

What we must realise is that rivers provide us with a valuable source of energy, sadly underused, and a natural habitat that supports some of our rarest and most beautiful wild flowers, animals and birds. Such an environment is unique and we need to preserve it. I hope we do.

The Tyne

Height at source: 1750 feet (North Tyne)
                        2150 feet (South Tyne)

Length: 62 miles
Runs from Peel Fell and Tynehead Fell to Tynemouth

Milton did the river a huge injustice when he called this the 'coaly Tyne'. The Tyne is a brighter and clearer stream than the Mersey, is immeasurably purer than the Thames, is only occasionally muddied like the Humber, and is at no time discoloured by coal.

from *Rivers of Great Britain* by Aaron Watson, 1892

The Tyne might be clear upstream towards its two sources, but a lot of murky water has passed under that famous Tyne Bridge since Mr Watson was upset by Mr Milton a century ago.

The North Tyne and the South Tyne meet at Hexham, each having travelled around thirty miles through lofty countryside. The North Tyne bubbles up from the slopes of Peel Fell on the edge of the Cheviot Hills near the Scottish border, and from there it tumbles down the hillsides, fortified by other streams, and through Kielder Forest which is the largest man-made forest in Western Europe. Here, in dense cover provided by the coniferous canopy, are pine martens, roe deer, red squirrels, rare butterflies, crossbills and owls. On the moors, feral goats roam among the cloudberry, and grouse shriek 'get-back, get-back'. No sooner has the stream penetrated the 250 square miles of larch, pine and spruce, than it enters the largest artificial reservoir in Britain – Kielder Water.

The bridge over the Tyne at Hexham dates from 1785 and offers fine views.

Completed in 1983, this vast reservoir holding around 200 million cubic metres of water is now a place for boating, windsurfing, fishing and exploring. There are camp and caravan sites, and organised pony trekking; in short, a leisure industry has sprung up in the middle of the forest.

At the top end of the reservoir, in the village of Kielder, is Kielder Castle. Built in the eighteenth century as a hunting lodge, it is now an information centre. There is also a National Rivers Authority Salmon Hatchery at Kielder which produces half a million juvenile salmon to stock the surrounding rivers.

Through the dam at the end of the reservoir the River North Tyne flows down through a valley where lead mining was once the major industry. Now forestry and sheep farming employ many of the locals in the market town of Bellingham, below which the River Rede runs into the North Tyne. There are trout and salmon to be caught in the river here, along with coarse fish.

The river is quite meaty by the time it reaches Wark, where cottages

The North Tyne is a swift-flowing river above the Roman settlement of Chesters.

Kielder Water, topped up by the North Tyne, is Britain's largest artificial reservoir.

surround a tranquil village green. In mediaeval times this was the capital of North Tynedale and a place where Scottish kings held court. The massive Wark Forest blankets the hills to the west of the river, and to the east are the disused quarries of Gunnerton Nick where whinstone and limestone grasslands give rise to rare wild flowers. On whinstone are hare's foot clover, parsley fern and dyer's greenweed, and on limestone are rock roses and meadow saxifrage.

Through the park of Chipchase Castle, a Jacobean house built round a mediaeval tower, the river travels another six miles before it comes to Chollerford, *Cilurnum* or Chesters to the Romans. The stone bridge dates from 1771, but this is also where

The South Tyne has its beginnings in Cumbria and then follows Hadrian's Wall for several miles before meeting up with the North Tyne near Hexham.

Hadrian's Wall crossed the North Tyne, and the remains of the bridge and the fort that guarded it will delight anyone interested in archaeology. The wall was built after the Emperor Hadrian's visit to Britain in AD 122. It was 73 miles long and had seventeen forts along its length, as well as smaller forts or 'mile-castles' at one-mile intervals to afford protection against the marauding Scots. Fifteen thousand men took seven years to build it.

The bathhouse by the river is especially fine and museums offer other treasures before the river flows a further three miles to meet the South Tyne at Hexham.

The South Tyne starts its life on the Cumbrian fells and, with the Pennine Way following its course, it journeys down through Garrigill past ruined lead mines to a town which was once the capital of the local mining industry, Alston. The highest market town in England at around 1000 feet, Alston is frequently cut off by snowfalls. During the early part of the nineteenth century the mines that had yielded lead, silver, zinc, iron, copper and fluorspar dwindled, and the railway went a century and a half later. Now the town is a centre for walkers.

For about 15 miles the river travels north before turning east at Haltwhistle, a small industrial town that lies in the shadow of Hadrian's Wall. Brown trout, sea trout and salmon can be fished here in what was once a coal-mining area.

The river follows Hadrian's Wall eastwards to Hexham where the North and South Tyne unite. The town grew up around the Abbey, built by St Wilfred in 678. The Crypt is all that remains of it today, built with stones from the Roman town of *Corstopitum*, downriver at Corbridge. Hexham is a popular centre for visitors and has some splendid old buildings including a fifteenth-century Moot Hall.

The river is wide here, with a couple of islands, and then snakes on past Corbridge between Ovingham on its north bank and Prudhoe to the south. Ovingham was the birthplace of the wood engraver Thomas Bewick (1753-1828) and its church bears a memorial to him. Prudhoe still has the remains of a Norman castle on its hill overlooking the river.

Wylam marks the tidal limit of the Tyne and it is also the birthplace of George Stephenson (1781–1848), the great railway pioneer. The cottage in which he was born is now a museum, and the railway offers a good view of the Tyne from here almost to the sea.

Past power stations at Ryton, the Tyne takes on the waters of the Derwent at Blaydon and slides into Newcastle Upon Tyne, with Gateshead on its south bank. Vast, cold and grey-brown, it passes under six bridges at the heart of the city, the most famous of which was built in 1928 and used as a model for the Sydney Harbour Bridge in Australia. Stephenson's high-level

Dated 1694, the seven-arched bridge at Corbridge withstood the 1771 Tyne floods.

The River Tyne, once as coal-black as Milton would have us believe, has now become one of the best salmon rivers in England, mainly thanks to a new system of sewage treatment which has intercepted most of the 180 outlets that formerly discharged into the river. This, coupled with tougher pollution regulations and an ability to use Kielder Water to add purer supplies, should continue to improve the state and colour of the Tyne's water.

Out of the city, between Wallsend and Hebburn, the river is undermined by road and pedestrian tunnels at Jarrow, forever associated with the 'hunger marches' that followed the closing of the Charles Palmer shipyards in 1933. Here, too, are the remains of a monastery, and St Paul's Church where the Venerable Bede (*c.* 673–735), the great Christian scholar, spent his life and wrote the first history of the English people in 731.

Tyne Docks was, until the liquidation of the Swan Hunter shipyards in 1993, the site of the biggest British ship repairing concern, and roll-on, roll-off ferries operate between here and Scandinavia. Coal, grain and oil terminals populate the banks of the Tyne, but so do industrial ruins - much of the riverside is desolate.

Through this incongruous mixture of history and industry, triumph and tragedy, the River Tyne flows to the North Sea at Tynemouth. Below the ruins of an eleventh-century priory the river is home to gulls, terns and skuas, and it bowls out into the briny between twin piers terminated with lighthouses.

road and rail bridge of 1849 still survives, as does the swing bridge of 1876 which turns on a central pivot.

Newcastle, capital of Northumbria, was originally a Roman fort by a river crossing near Hadrian's Wall. The 'new' castle was built in 1080 by William the Conqueror's eldest son, Robert Curthose. This castle was replaced by another in the twelfth century and part of it still stands by the cathedral.

Engineering and shipbuilding brought Newcastle its greatest commercial days in the nineteenth century, and the architecture reflects the changing fortunes of the city over the years.

Six bridges cross the Tyne in Newcastle including the towering road bridge of 1928.

The Wear

Height at source: 2150 feet
Length: 65 miles
Runs from Knoutberry Hill, County Durham, to Sunderland

The whole country was formerly studded with monasteries and with beautiful cities, founded therein by the Romans; but now, owing to the devastation of the Danes and Normans, it has nothing to allure the senses. Through it runs the Wear, a river of no mean width and tolerable rapidity. It flows into the sea, and receives ships, which are driven thither by the wind, into its tranquil bosom.

William of Malmesbury, a monk writing in the twelfth century

They were tough men, the miners of Killhope, whose wheel was powered by the infant Wear. Now a museum gives tourists a taster of their lifestyle.

Wild country breeds wild men, and up on the moors of Weardale it was a hearty breed who once mined 'the richest vein of lead ore in England'. Writing in 1892 John Geddie describes the miners as 'full of sturdy independence of thought, and free from many of the vices which mark their class elsewhere.' Now they are gone, but they have left behind them on Killhope Beck a 34-foot diameter waterwheel which is now part of a mining museum. Even before the river was considered strong enough to have its own name, its tributaries were considered strong enough to provide power for stone-crushing mills.

A whole collection of burns tumble down the slopes of these Durham peaks, through Weardale Forest. If you take the A689 from Alston in Cumbria you can come over the moors into Durham and follow the River Wear from its source right down through

Weardale. The Weardale Way takes pedestrians along a similar route.

Killhope Burn, Wellhope Burn and Burnhope Burn (dammed in 1930 to form a reservoir) unite along with dozens of their mates to become the River Wear at Wearhead, from where they flow eastwards to the sea.

The verdant dale is criss-crossed by dry-stone walls that pen the black-faced sheep, and peppered with old lead workings. Stone cottages make up

Durham Cathedral, dating from 1093, is the jewel in the crown of one of England's finest mediaeval cities.

a long chain of hamlets – places like Ireshopeburn where, in the latter half of the eighteenth century, John Wesley preached at five in the morning to crowds assembled under a thorn tree. The museum here gives you the feeling of what the place must have been like a century or two ago.

Through the village of St John's Chapel the Wear flows to Westgate and Eastgate, once the entrances to the Old Park where the Bishops of Durham would hunt. Men of coarser clay made Westgate a noted centre of cock-fighting, but today the bird life and wild flowers around Low Linn Falls at Eastgate are likely to provide more amusement, provided the nearby cement works does not engulf them in white dust.

Those expecting a completely picturesque dale of the Yorkshire variety might be disappointed by the amount of industry in Weardale, but the cement and steel and the limestone quarries from which lorries thunder can at least be left behind by those willing to scale the hills.

This is waterfall country. Nothing ranks with High Force on the River Tees, but smaller rivulets decorate the hillsides around Stanhope, where the iron ore mined further up the valley was brought when the blast furnace was built in 1845.

The ground yielded stone of greater beauty at Frosterley, three miles down-river. Frosterley marble was quarried here, but now there is precious little left. A kind of limestone, it blackens when polished to reveal multitudes of

Elvet Bridge in Durham City dates from 1160, though much of it was washed away in the great Tyne flood of 1771. In 1805 its width was doubled.

tiny fossils. The font in Eastgate parish church shows them off to perfection.

But the river shows off other things: the Wear is the finest sea trout river in England. Brown trout and coarse fish keep them company but they remain the greater prize, and from here down to Chester-le-Street they are angled for. To ensure the river never falls below minimum levels, a transfer tunnel carries water from Kielder Water reservoir on the Tyne to top up the Wear at Frosterley in times of drought.

Wolsingham is a good base-camp for Weardale exploration and from this stone-built town the river is deflected by the steelworks to dip southwards for

a few miles below Crook, at Escomb. It then reaches the town which, since the twelfth century, has been the seat of the Bishops of Durham – Bishop Auckland. The 'Prince Bishops' ruled like monarchs in this northernmost part of England for around 800 years, with their own armies, coinage and courts. They were soldiers and politicians as much as clergymen, and the grandeur of Auckland Castle, St Peter's Chapel and the parkland in which they are set reflects their status and power. The bishop who presides over Durham today has the best tied cottage in the whole of England.

The River Gaunless flows through

the Bishop's deer park to join the Wear, which then flows northwards for a spell until it encircles one of the finest mediaeval cities in England: Durham.

On a tree-fringed sandstone knoll that is almost an island stand Durham Castle (dating from 1070) and Durham Cathedral, begun in 1093 by Bishop William of Calais. Here lie the bones of St Cuthbert of Lindisfarne (c. 634–687) and of the Venerable Bede. Originally the castle was the site of a Saxon church built to house the remains of St Cuthbert – remains that gave him cult status because for centuries they seemed to be incorruptible. Whether it is to see the shrine of St Cuthbert, or one of the world's finest cathedrals, the pilgrims still journey to Durham in their millions.

The river, running through its tree-lined gorge, makes a moat around the castle and cathedral. On its banks, once a year, is held the Durham Miners Gala, when brass bands shatter the calm of the riparian air.

The Old Fulling Mill by the river is now a museum of archaeology, and by boat you can get a real feel of the geography of the place, passing under a series of bridges.

Now the river undergoes a series of ox-bows in a northerly direction past Finchale Priory and its tidal limit near Chester-le-Street to Washington. This new town was named after the Old Hall where ancestors of the first American president, famed for his truthfulness, once lived. While the town attracts commerce and residents, the wildfowl park attracts ducks, geese, waders, and over a hundred species of butterflies and moths. Handsome ferries take passengers from the wildfowl park to the river's final port of call on the east coast – Sunderland.

The town was founded on shipbuilding and coal mining, two industries that have suffered greatly in the recent recession, and derelict buildings and shattered foundations now follow the route of the river to the sea. Both trades continue to some extent, but the lofty cranes of shipyards are now challenged by office blocks as the town's commerce changes tack. Some delights have survived – like the Sunderland Empire, opened in 1907 by Vesta Tilley – and there are illuminations in autumn, a River Wear Trail that traces the old industries, and a steady stream of improvements to the environment. Sunderland may no longer be the biggest shipbuilding town in the world, but there is a rhyme that says: 'The Weardale men they have good hearts, and they are stiff as any tree.'

The River Wear flows into the North Sea between one pier carrying a lighthouse and another bearing a beacon. On some days it even gets cheered on its way when, over the sandy beaches of Roker (if the wind is in the west and the home team is winning) come the shouts of the supporters of Sunderland Association Football Club.

Many moorland burns unite at Wearhead to form the River Wear.

The Tees

Height at source: 2532 feet
Length: 70 miles
Runs from Cross Fell to Tees Mouth at Middlesbrough

It is a place of outstanding beauty – one of nature's masterpieces, you could say – and it is on my doorstep . . . I could not contemplate leaving the hills of Teesdale.

Hannah Hauxwell on High Force from *Hannah's North Country*, with Barry Cockroft, 1993

I have no claim to fame, except that of being Hannah Hauxwell's first dancing partner. Gentle of temperament, tough of spirit and enthralling company, she is the product of a life spent in isolation here in the northern Dales. For all the rivers in this book, the Tees has the most isolated source – just below the summit of Cross Fell in Cumbria which, at 2930 feet, is the highest peak in the Pennines.

Among boggy moorland, drenched by up to 90 inches of rainfall a year, Tees Head is seen only by hardy sheep, lonely grouse and determined walkers of the Pennine Way. Long-abandoned lead workings and dangerous mine shafts show signs of civilisation, though working up here in the nineteenth century must have been anything but civilised.

Smaller becks join the Tees as it snakes down the peaty slopes of the perversely treeless Milburn Forest to be met near one of the disused mines by Trout Beck, itself freshly topped up with the beer-brown waters of Moss Burn and Rough Sike; the names alone can make you shiver.

But inhospitable as this terrain may be for people and trees, it is a valuable habitat for alpine and sub-arctic wild flowers which find the conditions to their liking among the sugar limestone soil. In Teesdale grow spring gentians,

Alas, the protests of naturalists and conservationists could not stop the floral riches of Upper Teesdale being flooded to form Cow Green Reservoir in 1970.

One of England's most spectacular waterfalls when the River Tees is in full spate, High Force tumbles 70 feet over Great Whin Sill.

starry saxifrage, Teesdale violet and bog sandwort. There are rare lichens in this valley, newts and upland bumblebees, and other choice beauties found nowhere else in Britain. For this reason much of the area has been designated a nature reserve.

Alas, even that designation and the protests of thousands of conservationists could not stop a three-mile stretch of Upper Teesdale being turned into Cow Green Reservoir in 1970. About eight miles from its source the Tees is dammed to provide 9000 million gallons that will satisfy the demands of Teesside and enable the river below to be topped up in times of drought. The gentians that once grew beneath its waters now grow at its edges, thanks to the volunteers who set to with trowels and spades before the deluge.

As the Tees cascades out of the reservoir two things happen: it flows into Durham for the rest of its life, and in so doing tumbles over Cauldron Snout. This staircase of volcanic dolerite rock is 200 feet long, and though the dam above has done much to reduce the foaming of a cataract known to some sensitive Victorians as 'Cauldron Nose', it is still a spectacle. There are those who say that the dam has also reduced the effect of the 'Teesdale Roll', a massive wave of water that after sudden heavy downpours makes its way down the dale.

As the river descends so the scenery mellows with the reduction in altitude. It becomes softer, greener, delicious. But a surprise is just round the corner. The most spectacular waterfall on the Tees is High Force, five miles downstream of Cauldron Snout, where the river topples over the 70 foot crag of Great Whin Sill. Viewed when the river is in spate, the sound and the sight is awesome; I remember standing wide-eyed and open mouthed at the age of eight or nine as the water thundered into the stew pot below.

Trees appear on the banks now, and there are smaller rapids, runnels and waterfalls down a valley dotted with hamlets. Low Force provides its own spectacle, and numerous tributaries bump down the sides of the valley to join the river.

Middleton-in-Teesdale is the first town of note. A small one, it was the centre of the lead mining industry from the seventeenth to the nineteenth century and a Quaker stronghold. Now it is a centre for walkers.

The River Lune flows into the Tees to the east of Middleton, having passed through two of its own reservoirs, and Eggleston Burn joins the fray near the pleasant village of Romaldkirk.

Nature reserves abound. Shipley and Great Woods at Eggleston shelter red squirrels, and the River Balder meets the Tees at Hannah Hauxwell's village of Cotherstone. There are trout and grayling in the clear waters and redstarts and roe deer in Deepdale Wood near Barnard Castle.

The castle itself is now a ruin, built in the twelfth century to safeguard the river crossing. The view from the Round Tower is said to have inspired Sir Walter Scott to write *Rokeby*, and Charles Dickens stayed at the King's Head when working on *Nicholas Nickleby*. Was Dotheboys Hall nearby?

Today Barnard Castle is a pleasant market town which, aside from its market cross and handsome houses, boasts the Bowes Museum, housed in a most spectacular French-style chateau.

Flooding is not unknown in Barnard Castle, and on the wall of the old mill by the bridge is the water-level mark of the 1881 floods. The 1771 floods knocked down part of the bridge and destroyed several cottages.

From here past the ruins of Egglestone Abbey, the Tees passes through a rocky gorge, and at the edge of Rokeby Park is 'The Meeting of the Waters', where the River Greta flows into the Tees.

Down a dale dotted with white-painted cottages (the Duke of Cleveland liked to know where his tenants were, even in the dark), the river makes its way for miles, past hamlets and woods and pastures, and chameleon-like begins to change its character. The bubbling dales stream is about to become an industrial river and over the next few miles it must prepare itself for a shock.

Wriggling like a snake, it passes to the south of Darlington and three major abstraction points that will supply Darlington and Teesside with their water. Coarse fish join the trout and grayling now.

Yarm is the tidal limit of the river and, because the Tees makes a great loop here, it has often been flooded; the market hall is engraved with the flood levels of 1771 and 1881. Plans are underway for a flood defence scheme to prevent such a recurrence. Today the town is dominated by a stupendous viaduct carrying the railway over the river and roads. It is a fitting memorial to the fact that the first meeting of the first public railway in the world was held in the George and Dragon Inn on 12 February 1820.

Swollen on the outskirts of town by the River Leven, the Tees now has no

Barnard Castle, built by Guy de Balliol in the twelfth century to safeguard the river-crossing. Later his nephew Bernard rebuilt it – hence the name.

escape. It must flow between Stockton-on-Tees and Billingham to the north and Middlesbrough to the south. Downstream of Stockton the river could only be crossed by ferry boat until the Transporter Bridge, slung from cables high above the water, was built in 1911.

Until the early part of this century the Tees was a famous salmon river. Ten thousand were netted in a single season in 1867, but by 1970 the lower reaches of the river and estuary were among the most polluted in Britain; the salmon were long gone.

The estuary is still in a parlous state, but improved sewage treatments and long overdue control over the release of pollutants by steel industries and the largest concentration of chemical and petro-chemical works in Europe have, at last, resulted in the appearance of one or two salmon and sea trout. Reed beds are being planted to provide 'Root Zone' treatment that will further purify the water released from chemical plants.

The Tees Barrage, to be constructed below Stockton, will maintain water levels upstream and reduce the encroachment of pollution from chemical plants downstream. All treated

The Middlesbrough Transporter Bridge built in 1911 to take traffic over the river by cable car.

sewage effluent will be expelled below the barrier which should also help to reduce the risk of flooding.

You end up asking yourself why all this has taken so long and the answer is, as always, money. The National Rivers Authority for this area talks about 'the occasional otter and kingfisher'. Surprisingly among this despoliation at the end of the river's journey to the sea are Seal Sands and Tees Mouth which are amazingly rich in bird life. Waders, divers and ducks winter here, including five per cent of Europe's shelduck population. There are snow buntings and shore larks, and reed beds a little inland that boast bearded tits, reed warblers and bitterns. The once pure river slides greasily out into Tees Bay past colonies of grey seals, and mingles with the sea alongside sand dunes sprouting bloody cranesbill and purple milk-vetch. We really don't deserve them.

Considering that the Tees estuary has the largest concentration of chemical and petro-chemical works in Europe it is not surprising that pollution is a problem. But work is underway to purify the water in the reedbeds.

The Wharfe

Height at source: 1500 feet
Length: 60 miles
Runs from Oughtershaw to Cawood

If ever one was metamorphosed into a river, and could choose one's own size, it would be out of all doubt more prudent and delightful to be Wharfe than Rhône.

John Ruskin, 1885

I would rather be the Wharfe than any other river I know, but then I was born in Wharfedale. Anyone jaded enough to believe that the English countryside is not what it was should journey to the source of the Wharfe and follow it down dale for a day. Described by Harry Speight in 1900 as being 'the Queen of Yorkshire Dales', Wharfedale is still a place of unspoiled beauty in its upper reaches. From its source high above Langstrothdale, down to its union with the Ouse at Cawood, near Selby, the Wharfe passes through some of England's most robust and refreshing terrain.

It is that rarity: the river with an interesting source. It starts life as Oughtershaw Beck in the bottom of a moorland valley, fed by streams that spurt from the opposing fells of Cam Rakes and Oughtershaw Side like burst white veins. No trickle this, but a brimming beck with fast-flowing water that lives up to its Saxon name: Wharfe is derived from *Guerf*, meaning swift. Just yards away from the source of the Wharfe is the source of the Ribble

which starts its journey by flowing in the opposite direction.

The fells around here are rolling rather than craggy, tinged with the russet of reeds in autumn and peppered at all times of year with

hardy sheep, blotched with red on their matted wool. Dry limestone walls and ditches criss-cross the boggy land and no white lines stain the single-track road – the staining around here is left to farm animals.

The air is clear and the water amber in Langstrothdale – the valley that carries the stripling Wharfe from the village of Beckermonds down as far as Bucken.

Oughtershaw itself is nothing more than a hamlet with a rustic farm where sheep cluster in the dank shade of an ash tree, sheltered from biting wind, driving rain or scorching sun by a moss-covered dry stone wall. There is a monolith of stone by the road, carved with a cross and the inscription *VR 1887*. Queen Victoria's Golden Jubilee was celebrated with this simple but permanent memorial.

Up here where, as a Yorkshireman of my acquaintance says, 'men are men and sheep are nervous', the urban-looking Victorian church seems out of place, which is probably why it is now a youth centre. The serious travellers are on foot – everyone not wearing a battered old mac, flat hat and herding sheep is dressed in bright kagoul, boots that look as though they mean business, and waterproof leggings. They probably have a long walk ahead of them – the Pennine Way passes the top of the Wharfe on Cam Fell, and the Dales Way runs right through Wharfedale from Ilkley, with Windermere as its ultimate destination.

Soon the pastures become less reedy and there are attempts at making hay. At the side of the road Oughtershaw Hall stands behind spiked iron gates flanked with huge stone pillars. Here is the perfect setting for a Victorian thriller – a rambling house with mullioned windows built in 1850 for the Woodd family of Hampstead who owned the estate.

Another stream joins Oughtershaw Beck now. Green Field Beck has come down an adjacent valley through the

At Yockenthwaite the river tumbles over a series of elegant shallow waterfalls. Here the limestone is worn smooth by thousands of years of cascading torrents.

village of Beckermonds. At the marriage of the two, the Wharfe is born and flows on through the valley known as Langstrothdale, tumbling over convoluted limestone outcrops to make waterfalls that any landscape gardener would sigh for. Sepia tinted is the water on account of its peaty origins. It is described by locals as being the colour of pale ale, and turns to creamy foam when it hurtles over rocks by the side of the road.

Yockenthwaite is the first village on the Wharfe. There isn't a lot of it – a few long, low, grey stone houses with mullioned windows, and a bevy of

barns – and the neat limestone pack-horse bridge sticks in the memory more than the rough circle of stones a few yards from the Wharfe that is said to date from the Bronze Age.

Looking down the valley, Great Whernside looms ahead. This is one of the largest peaks in the Pennines at 2414 feet and, as you journey towards it, you come to Hubberholme.

Take a pint of ale in the George Inn and then walk across the old stone bridge to the Church of St Michael and All Angels. The inn building, at one time the vicarage, stayed in the ownership of the Church until 1965. Each

New Year's Day the vicar would preside over a crude parliament when the 'Poor Pasture' was let to the peasantry. It still happens today but the term 'peasantry' is, perhaps, less applicable.

The church is mainly twelfth century but even if you are not into ecclesiastical architecture you can savour its delights. Rough stone Norman archways line the knave and the feeling is of a beautifully constructed barn. Not surprising when you discover that the church began its life as a forest chapel. It is a low building and the square tower is squat, as if to duck beneath the wind.

Guide books praise the rood loft that dates from 1558, but have a closer look at the oak pews and chairs, now as smooth as silk with years of wear. They were made by 'The Mouseman' – Robert Thompson of Kilburn in North Yorkshire – who signed each of his pieces with the carving of a mouse. He died in 1955, but signed furniture is still produced by the firm that carries his name.

Hubberholme possesses the first hostelry on the journey down Wharfedale – the George Inn – and also the first church. In former times the inn building was the vicarage and an old stone bridge links it with the Norman church on the river's north bank.

For a small village Kettlewell is blessed with more than its fair share of inns. They offer sustenance to those attempting the nearby peak of Great Whernside.

Grassington, the capital of Upper Wharfedale, was granted a charter for a market and fair in 1282. Today tourists are its main industry but it remains unruffled by change.

St Michael and All Angels is a favourite church of mine, and I am in good company. On the wall at the back of the nave is a plaque which reads:

Remember J. B. Priestley OM 1894–1984, author and dramatist whose ashes are buried nearby. He loved the Dales and found 'Hubberholme one of the smallest and pleasantest places in the world.'

The village names around here give you a potted history of the place. Hubberholme was named as a compliment to the Viking prince Hubba who, with his brothers, wrested Northumbria from the English. The next village, Buckden, was once surrounded by the deer-filled forest of Langstrothdale, where buck were regularly hunted (the pub is the Buck Inn), while Starbotton is Anglo-Saxon for stony bottom.

Never was a place so aptly named for in 1686 'an earthquake and a violent and dreadful tempest of thunder, hail and rain' washed away bridges and houses, leaving the village no more than a pile of stones. Some houses survived, others were 'filled with gravel to the chamber windows'. There followed what must rank as one of the earliest national appeals, for money came from as far afield as Cambridgeshire. Today the village is tidy and trim with cottages in finest livery to attract those who would rather spend their summers in the Dales than the Dordogne.

The flood did great damage to other villages down the valley – villages like Kettlewell, which is Norse for bubbling spring, a name that still suits it well. Small this village may be but with the Racehorses, the Bluebell and the King's Head it is unlikely to run dry. It is a pleasing village to explore and a popular centre for walking – a sort of base camp for Great Whernside, down which Cam Beck runs to join the Wharfe.

So quiet is the village now (apart from the activity of walkers) that it is difficult to picture it as a hive of industry, but in 1838 there were lead mines all around on the fells, no less than five inns, a cotton mill, a beer-house, three schools, three blacksmiths and all the other trades such activity could employ.

Lower down the valley, the River Skirfare joins the Wharfe. It has been flowing through nearby Littondale and its villages of Litton and Arncliffe.

Charles Kingsley's *The Water Babies* was inspired by Littondale, and Tom the chimney sweep slipped into the River Skirfare at the bottom of Bridge End House garden in Arncliffe to become a water baby.

There are dangers of equal gravity to be found down the road at Kilnsey Crag. Looming over the road, this lime-stone scar, 170 feet high with a 40-foot overhang, looks like a gigantic unfinished sphinx, over whose rugged nose climbers forever seem to be dangling. There is a trout farm along-side it now for those who use a thinner line and, in late August or early September, the locals gather with folk from far afield for Kilnsey Show with its sheepdog trials and dry stone walling competition, held in the

The River Wharfe below Kilnsey Crag has always been good fishing water. In the nineteenth century 1200 trout could be caught in a season.

meadows near the river.

The valley runs wider now and is carpeted with meadows on which cattle graze. The river is wider too; gentle and bubbling in summer but trans-formed into a raging torrent when assisted by winds and heavy rain.

You can travel on either side of the river by road at this point, choosing whether to go through Threshfield or to cross the bridge at Kilnsey and go through Conistone (the prettier of the two) to reach the capital of Upper Wharfedale, Grassington.

'The place isn't what it was,' said the lady in the Dales Bookshop, casting an eye through her shop window at the flocks of tourists. But even if Grassington is rather busy, it seems to have the right kind of tourists, and its atmosphere is generally unimpaired by their presence.

You can spend hours here, exploring for hidden 'folds' – yards sur-rounded by small houses that at one time were lived in by the lead miners who came from Wales and Cornwall to ply their trade. Now they are more likely to be holiday homes. But this is no bucolic Benidorm. Grassington still has dignity, charm and history a-plenty.

The Black Death wiped out a quarter of the population of the village in 1349 – the kind of thing you will discover if you visit the Upper Wharfedale Museum in the village square. Plett's Barn, in which John Wesley preached in 1780, still stands – it is now a mountaineering shop. One cottage marks the spot of Grassington's theatre, where Edmund Kean performed in 1807 under his real name of Carter, and for the morbid, the flower shop up the main street was once the 'smidy' owned by Tom Lee who murdered the local doctor in Grass Wood in 1766 and dumped his body in the Wharfe. Executed at York Castle for his misdeeds, Lee's body was hung on a gibbet at the site of the murder. They still call it Gibbet Hill. Today Grass Wood is concerned more with wildlife than wild life. It is a rare example of a limestone wood.

A creamery, a worsted mill and then a cotton mill stood by Linton Falls in earlier times.

'The Smidy', once home to murderer Tom Lee, is now a flower shop.

The Dales Bookshop has *One Hundred Things to See on a Walk through Grassington*, sold in aid of local charities and packed with 'gosh factor'.

As for me, I am never happier than when sitting outside the Devonshire Arms in the village square, with a pint of ale and a ploughman's lunch, watching the world go by.

Purists favour the village of Linton, just across the river. Much less com-mercialised, it has a village green cut in half by a stream over which pass hump-backed stone bridges for pedes-trians and traffic. Twin avenues of lime trees offer dappled shade in summer, and ducks preen themselves on the grass. Grey stone houses and farms encircle the green, along with a row of alms houses known as the Fountaine Hospital – complete with dome over a central gate. These were built by a local benefactor in 1721 for 'six poor men and women'. So grand is the architecture that it is not surprising that some attribute the design to Sir John Vanbrugh.

Just down the road are Linton Falls which form a Niagara of a waterfall after heavy rain. They tumble in a wide cataract caused by the North Craven Fault, and the sound of falling water is deafening if you stand on the wooden bridge when the river is in full spate.

Linton Mill was here, but eventually was demolished and replaced by a small, select development of riverside houses whose windows overlook the swift, deep water.

We go downriver now to Burnsall, with its handsome five-arched bridge. The Red Lion presides over the bridge, and there are grassy banks on either side of the river where picnickers can unpack their hampers.

From here down to Bolton Abbey is my favourite part of Wharfedale. The land is gently rolling, the grass is lime-green velvet, and rich green trees in clumps, coppices and woods run over it like a thick pelt. It is generous countryside, with a wholesome river at its heart.

Downstream from Burnsall, and to the north of the river, you will come to Appletreewick, a collection of neat, grey stone houses that are strung along the road. Tiny now, the village was given a charter to hold a fair in 1311. It later became known as the Onion Fair. Nowadays Appletreewick is a place of more energetic entertainment, for where the River Dibb joins the Wharfe there are national canoe slalom championships.

Just out of the village, down a one-mile road that terminates at its gates, is Parcevall Hall, a stone-built

Built in 1612, Burnsall Bridge replaces all previous bridges, which were washed away by the river. It was the gift of a local boy who became Lord Mayor of London – Sir William Craven – born in Appletreewick in 1548.

The Wharfe

Elizabethan house that once sheltered a notorious highwayman called William Nevison. Now it shelters anyone who wants to go on Diocesan retreat, but the gardens are open to all visitors in spring and summer. A handsome house with mullioned windows, it looks out across a series of terraced gardens to the opposite side of the valley – allowing breathtaking views guaranteed to result in peace of mind.

Lower down the valley is the ruin of Barden Tower. Originally a twelfth-century hunting lodge, it was rebuilt and extended by Henry Clifford, tenth Lord of the Manor of Skipton in the fifteenth century. The Cliffords were Lancastrians who lost their estates during the Wars of the Roses. Henry was restored to his position on the accession of Henry VII but having been brought up in a shepherd's family in Cumberland, the Shepherd Lord, as he was called, preferred Barden to his

Appletreewick dozes peacefully in the summer sun. It is hard to believe that in mediaeval times it was more bustling than Burnsall and had a great four-day fair.

Church services are still held in part of Bolton Abbey, an Augustinian priory dating from the twelfth century. The dissolution brought about its downfall.

main seat at Skipton. Here he could dabble in his favourite pursuits of astronomy and alchemy. The tower again fell into disrepair until it was restored by Lady Anne Clifford in 1659. Now it is a shell, but one picturesque enough to attract artists at all times of year.

Perhaps the one place that draws more visitors than any other in this part of the valley is Bolton Abbey. Really a twelfth-century priory, it suffered, like most others, during the Reformation. It stands like an elegant skeleton, proud in its ruination, on the banks of the Wharfe and has for centuries inspired poets such as Ruskin and Wordsworth, and artists like Turner and Landseer whose *Bolton Abbey in Olden Times* hangs at Chatsworth. The Bolton Abbey Estate, like Chatsworth, belongs to the Duke

of Devonshire, having passed down through the line of the Clifford family who bought the land when the Augustinian canons were deprived of their property.

Long before that, in the twelfth century, Romilly was the name that held sway in these parts. I was brought up on the story that Alice Romilly gave the lands of Bolton to the Augustinian canons after her son had died in the Strid. You will find this treacherous narrowing of the Wharfe in Strid Wood, just down from the Abbey. The water boils through the overhanging rocks and it is here that Alice's son, the boy Egremond, while attempting to jump the river, was held back by his dog's leash and fell to his death in the turbulent water. Alice, it is said, never recovered from her grief. There are nature trails here now – stick to them rather than trying to jump what is now rather more than a 'stride'.

Part of Bolton Abbey is still used as a church, and on the road outside is the Cavendish Memorial – a sort of miniature Albert Memorial which is really a fountain. It was erected to the memory of Lord Frederick Charles Cavendish who was murdered within six hours of his arrival in Ireland as Chief Secretary in 1882.

On a brighter note, this was the parish of Revd William Carr for fifty-four years. He died in 1843 but during his tenure he opened up much of the countryside for walkers, and had the honour of having bred the Craven Heifer in 1807. Many a pub in the area is named after this beast which weighed 150 stone and was sold for £200. A snip! On the Arches Farm, where Carr lived, the Dukes Barn is said still to have the wide door needed to accommodate the heifer's girth.

You will find a Craven Heifer pub in Addingham, three miles downstream of Bolton Abbey. Addingham was once a thriving mill town – my mother worked in Low Mill making knitting wool until the war of 1939–45, then the attention turned to khaki and airforce blue, as well as munitions. Sadly she is not old enough to relate stories of the Luddite revolts that were rife in this area in the early nineteenth century. Today Addingham is less industrious, contenting itself with farming and related activities.

And so to Ilkley, the first town on the Wharfe. It is where I was born, so you will forgive my passion for it. Everyone knows it for its anthem 'On Ilkla Moor Baht 'At', but the Romans knew it as Olicana. They have all been there: Romans, Saxons and Brigantes, leaving their marks, but the Victorians left the most tangible legacy when they decided that the chalybeate waters emerging from moorland springs were beneficial to the health. Ilkley became a spa town in the nineteenth century and thrived. Hydropathic establishments sprang up everywhere; once there were fifteen of them – some of them still stand – and visitors flocked to take the iron-rich waters.

Ilkley is a pretty town with the river on its northern side. From the Old Bridge, built in 1673, we used to watch trout nosing gently upstream – perfectly camouflaged against the ochre-coloured rocks below. On the pebbly shores below the New Bridge where willow trees overhang the opposite bank, we would tickle bullheads under their chins and coax them into jam-jars – far easier to catch than wary catfish – and occasionally a crayfish would nip you on the ankle from under a rock. But fishermen want meatier prey, and the Wharfe today offers trout

The Wharfe is at its strongest and most threatening at the Strid – now far more than a stride wide after raging waters have worn away its gritstone boundaries.

and grayling from Ilkley up as far as Buckden, and plenty of chub, perch, dace, gudgeon and roach. The salmon that once ran the river are now a rarity.

From the river you can look up to the heather-clad moor, afire with bracken in autumn, and see the Cow and Calf Rocks. Geologists will talk of glacial activity, but the climbers and I know full well that the smaller Calf was dislodged from the Cow by the foot of the giant Rombald leaping across the valley. It is Rombald's Moor after all.

Over both of these chunks of millstone grit you will find Edwardian and Victorian graffiti. There are other rocks around here that show the handiwork of earlier civilisations: the Swastika Stone above Heber's Ghyll is thought to be Yorkshire's oldest rock carving

(prehistoric is the nearest they get to dating it) and there are Cup and Ring Stones on the moor that are said to date back to the Bronze Age.

The Manor House is later, dating from the sixteenth and seventeenth centuries. It stands on the site of the Roman fort next to the parish church of All Saints where I sang in my youth as a choirboy. The Saxon crosses that once stood outside are now housed under the tower of this handsome church that dates in part from the thirteenth century.

On the north side of the river is Middleton, named after the ancient family that gives its name to Middleton Woods – superb bluebell woods that run down to the banks of the Wharfe. Look across the valley from Middleton and you will see White Wells, a white-

Before the days of the spraycan, travellers picked out their names with a cold chisel, in luxurious copperplate, on the Cow and Calf Rocks.

painted building on the moors. Squire Middleton erected the open-air baths here in 1756; roofs were added a century later to allow the Victorians to plunge in comfort. Take a look at the icy waters there now and you will marvel at their bravery.

The Heather Spa, as Ilkley was called, now attracts tourists more interested in boating on the water below the Old Bridge than drinking the moorland springs. But it still has that air of prosperity that is, in part, a legacy of the wool merchants who moved here at the turn of the last century to escape their daily life in the mills of Leeds and Bradford.

From the town the river flows on past Denton Hall, a stately and picturesque pile. This was once the home of Sir Thomas Fairfax who opposed the King in the Civil War, and as commander-in-chief of the Parliamentary armies, was responsible for the victory at Naseby. Later disillusioned with the cause, he helped

The Old Bridge at Ilkley no longer takes traffic, only folk on foot who have time to look over its parapet and spot speckled trout nosing their way upstream.

Ilkley and the Wharfe Valley from Cow and Calf Rocks. There used to be a Bull but it was quarried – an early blow for feminism?

restore Charles II to the throne. Denton Hall is now the headquarters of a computer firm.

From here you can go on to Burley in Wharfedale, described by the historian Thomas Whittaker in the last century as being 'a delightful village, though contaminated physically and morally by a cotton mill'. The contamination has now disappeared and the river wends on to Otley, the birthplace of the cabinet-maker Thomas Chippendale.

Otley is a market town, full of alleyways and courtyards. Otley Show is famous among the locals as being the first of the year, in May, and for always being wet. Not true – it just seems that way as you walk among steaming Friesians and blackface sheep.

In the churchyard at Otley you will find an intriguing monument: a scale model of Bramhope Tunnel, on the nearby railway line from Leeds to Harrogate. It commemorates the thirty men who died between 1845 and 1849 while the tunnel was being made.

The valley is broader now, gentler in feel than it was twenty miles ago. Across its river banks gaze imposing buildings like Farnley Hall, just above the confluence of Wharfe and Washburn, and then Arthington Hall, below Pool in Wharfedale where you can see the Arthington Viaduct that takes the railway across the river. It may not be quite as spectacular as the Ribblehead Viaduct on the Settle to Carlisle line but it is not far short.

Harewood House, home of the Earl of Harewood, is the most stately home in these parts. Built by John Carr and Robert Adam for Edwin Lascelles, it was completed in 1771 and has a park designed by Lancelot 'Capability' Brown, and furniture by local lad Thomas Chippendale. What more could the gentry ask for? Today visitors

Denton Hall, near Ilkley, was designed by John Carr of York and built in 1778 on the site of the earlier hall owned by Sir Thomas Fairfax, Cromwell's Commander-in-Chief.

The coming of the railway gave new life to the Dales but it also brought casualties. This monument in Otley churchyard commemorates the men who died building the Bramhope Tunnel.

can enjoy masses of rhododendrons and a bird garden into the bargain.

The Wharfe is forging ahead now. The moors seem an age behind as the river powers on past Wetherby, famous for its racecourse and with a superb bridge spanning the river below a weir, to Boston Spa and Thorp Arch, linked by another handsome stone bridge. Boston Spa takes its name from the mineral springs discovered in 1774 – the bath-house survives as the headquarters of an angling club.

You might think that the water of the River Wharfe is not what it was but at Tadcaster, where the water flows over magnesian limestone, the brewing industry still thrives. Those arch rivals, Samuel Smith and John Smith, will testify to this, along with that other local brewer, Mr Tetley. Back as far as 1378 there were five registered innkeepers in Tadcaster, but it was not until the nineteenth century that John Smith started his brewery producing

'clear beer'. After his death, a family row split the firm in two, and the town still reeks of their rivalry – on brewing days, that is.

Spanning the river here is the Virgin Bridge, built by Hudson of York to carry the Leeds to York railway in 1846. Why the Virgin Bridge? Well, the railway industry had over-reached itself, the cash was not forthcoming, and the track was never laid. But the bridge still stands. Below Tadcaster Weir, the river becomes tidal and fishermen can add flounder and eels to their bag of trout. It is a good place to leave the Wharfe. The river is broad and burly now and in a few miles, at Cawood, it will meet the Ouse to become more muscular still.

The last word belongs to Tom Bradley, who wrote for the *Yorkshire Weekly Post* in 1890: 'At the confluence of the Wharfe with the Ouse there is nothing of the picturesque to recommend it to any but a passing notice.'

The Trent

Height at source: 900 feet
Length: 170 miles
Runs from Biddulph Moor to Blacktoft Sand on the Humber

'Yes, the Town Clerk will see you.' In I went.
He was, like all Town Clerks, from north of Trent;
A man with bye-laws busy in his head
Whose mayor and council followed where he led.

from 'The Town Clerk's Views' by Sir John Betjeman, 1948

On the edge of Biddulph Moor, near the source of the Trent, there is little indication of the industry that will soon flank its banks.

There is still a feeling among English people that the real divide between northerners and southerners is not the frequently quoted Watford, but the River Trent. And there are those who suggest that there is more to it than the bluntness of the locals; the Trent is considered by some to be the climatic dividing line between northern and southern bird populations.

No one would doubt its reputation as an industrial river – from the banks of the Trent come coal, electricity and pottery – but the Trent also deserves sympathy for the way in which it has been ill-treated over the years.

By the mid-1960s parts of the Trent had become little more than open sewers, thanks to lack of capital expenditure during and after the Second World War. Incapable of producing a drinkable supply, the water was used only by the likes of the Central Electricity Generating Board for cooling purposes. Between the mid-sixties and late seventies the water was improved to its present level, thanks to

On one of the crags near the source of the Trent stands Mow Cop Castle, built as a folly in 1760 by Randle Wilbraham. This was the time when the local gentry could decorate the countryside as they saw fit. The ruined castle was a frivolous ornament, nothing more.

journey south and ultimately northwards and eastwards to flow, instead, into the Humber.

Past the aptly named hamlet of Rock End, the infant Trent makes its way through woodland to flow into the Knypersley Reservoir. When it emerges at the other end of this sheet of water under a road bridge, the Ordnance Survey map condescends to admit to it being the 'Head of Trent'. It then runs through its last stretch of reed-banked moorland to reach the centre of the city to which it gives its name: Stoke-on-Trent.

In 1910 the 'Five Towns' made famous by local novelist Arnold Bennett were joined together to make one large town. Hanley, Burslem, Tunstall, Longton and Stoke were linked with a sixth town, Fenton, to form Stoke-on-Trent.

Pottery has been made here for over 4000 years – shards have been found that date back to Neolithic times. In the seventeenth century readily available supplies of clay, coal and water resulted in a prodigious output of earthenware and stoneware. A real boost was given to the area known as 'The Potteries' after 1657 when tea was introduced to Britain and the gentry needed vessels in which to make their infusions and something out of which to drink the resulting liquid. It was in Stoke-on-Trent that the tea-set was invented. But it was in the eighteenth century that the area became famous as the home of Wedgwood, Minton, Copeland and Spode.

Josiah Wedgwood was born in

the utilisation of sewage treatment plants and greater controls over points of discharge. There is one snag to this improvement: in the clearer waters fish are harder to catch.

The source of the Trent is at Biddulph Moor in Staffordshire, close to the Cheshire border. In truth there are a number of streams at its beginnings, but it is generally accepted that the spout which juts out of a wall bearing the date 1935 is the true

source. It is a good, clean start anyway for the third longest river in England, after the Severn and the Thames.

Biddulph Moor is the name of the village, dominated by rocky crags that tower over some of its houses. Nearby Biddulph is a small colliery town surrounded by moorland.

From here it is barely 30 miles to the Mersey, but geological configurations make it impossible for the river to travel in that direction and it begins a

Barely seven or eight miles from its source the river is about to shed its rural image and enter Stoke-on-Trent.

Burslem in 1730 and set up his own business in 1759. With the Yorkshire-born John Flaxman as his main designer he became a master potter famous for his range of 'Queen's Ware', beloved of Queen Charlotte, and later of the blue and white Wedgwood we know today.

Where once both raw materials and finished product had to be carted by pack-horses and wagons on miry tracks or, at best, on privately owned and maintained turnpike roads, a canal network facilitated easier importation of china clays from the west country. It also meant that pottery could be

exported with fewer breakages. James Brindley was the driving force behind 365 miles of canal. A Derbyshire man who was barely literate, Brindley's solution to difficult problems was to go to bed and work them out.

Several pottery companies open their buildings to visitors nowadays,

On leaving Stoke-on-Trent the river gains some respite at Trentham Park Gardens, flowing in sight of rose gardens and ornamental shrubs.

including Wedgwood, Spode and Royal Doulton, and you can still see bottle ovens where the pottery was once fired at places like the Gladstone Pottery Museum in Longton.

The Trent and Mersey Canal and the River Trent meet in the centre of Stoke, the canal having flowed through Wedgwood's original pottery site which he christened Etruria, an old name for that part of Italy we now call Tuscany. There is no similarity in landscape. The river and the canal eventually part to the south of Stoke and the river is offered a brighter prospect than the city it has just left – Trentham Park Gardens.

Lancelot 'Capability' Brown designed the 400 acres of parkland,

William Nesfield was responsible for a large Italian garden and Sir Charles Barry built the formal gardens for the Duke of Sutherland on the encouragement of his wife, Harriet, Mistress of the Robes to Queen Victoria. (The Duke and Duchess went on to rebuild Cliveden in 1850 – see page 79 – using Sir Charles Barry as their architect.)

If only the Trent had been as clean in 1905 as it is today the house itself might have been saved. The Duke of that time apparently found the filth and the stench of the river too much to bear. He moved out, and the house was later demolished.

The main road, the river, the canal and the railway play nip-and-tuck over the next few miles past a sewage works, the present-day Wedgwood factory at Barlaston and a power station before passing by Tittensor Chase and on through Stone. It is an old town that can boast being the birthplace of John Jervis, one of England's most famous admirals, and Peter de Wint, the painter, was born here in 1784.

The Trent valley which leads out of Stone offers countryside views that are a tremendous contrast to the preceding industrial landscape.

There are chub, roach, bream and perch to be caught in the Trent here, but that is hardly the kind of unparalleled piscatorial richness you would expect on the doorstep of Izaak Walton, author of *The Compleat Angler*. He was born in 1593 three miles down the lane from Stone at Shallowford, and his cottage near the Meece Brook is now a museum. He was sixty when the

Gladstone Pottery Museum at Longton, where brick-built bottle ovens nestle side by side, gives a flavour of life in the potteries in the nineteenth century.

book was first published, and died, aged ninety, in 1683. I like the sound of Walton, who asked his readers to be careful not to cause undue suffering to the frogs they used as bait.

Past Hopton Heath, the site of a Civil War battle in 1643, the River Trent is joined by the River Sow on the edge of the Earl of Lichfield's country estate, Shugborough Park. United, they then flow under the elegant arches of the sixteenth-century Essex Bridge. Shugborough has been the seat of the Earls of Lichfield since William Anson bought the estate in 1624. The Sow encloses it on one side and the Trent on another; the house, gardens and grounds are worth a visit. The river, having paid its call, sticks with its old friend the Trent and Mersey Canal and flows past the northern edge of one of the country's most important heathlands, Cannock Chase.

As if to emphasise the north-south divide of the Trent, Cannock Chase is seen as the transition between lowland heath and northern moor. Heather and bilberry are here, as are siskin, redpoll, nightjar, long-eared owl, whinchat, stonechat and, in winter, great grey shrike. There are butterflies such as the pearl-bordered fritillary, and a wide variety of fungi and oak trees up to 300 years old. Wildfowl overwinter at Brocton Pool. The Chase is a site of amazing riches, where deer browse among trees, shrubs and heathland.

Passing the outskirts of Rugeley the water of the Trent is used as a coolant for twin power stations – the coal, the water and the electricity all existing on

At Alrewas the Trent and Mersey Canal ducks under a series of hump-backed bridges before joining the Trent. Alrewas was once famed for its eel fishery and for baskets woven from riverside osiers.

one site. River and canal go their separate ways for the next few miles, flowing either side of King's Bromley, and the Trent takes on the water of the Rivers Blithe and Swarbourn. At the picturesque village of Alrewas, replete with black and white half-timbered thatched cottages, the canal and the river join together, the canal having ducked under a series of tiny hump-backed bridges. The two then separate again and flow northwards either side of the A38(T). With the Rivers Mease and Tame joining its flow, the Trent is

well swollen when it reaches Burton upon Trent.

Again the river does its bit for a series of mighty power stations, but Burton upon Trent is known for one thing above all others – beer. You might be concerned that the Trent's less than sparkling waters should be finding their way into your frothing tankard of Burton ale. They are not. The water for the brewing industry comes from wells and springs below ground. There is now little trace of Burton Abbey, founded a thousand years ago. Maybe the monks were the first brewers.

Ale was certainly brewed here in the Middle Ages, and today there is more than a trace of hops and malt in the air with names like Worthington and Bass continuing the tradition. In the nineteenth century Michael Bass became Lord Burton. A nice touch.

The flood plain of the Trent around Burton has been engulfed on several occasions – notably in 1795, 1875 and 1947. Then, in the 1960s, a scheme of flood defences was devised which will hopefully limit future damage. In the centre of the town the river divides and some of its water flows down a channel known as the Silverway to create

Andresey Island. This, and the smaller island known as the Broad Holme, are part of Burton's Trent Washlands, a leisure and wildlife area with wetland flora and bird life. There is a regatta on the river each July.

Above Burton upon Trent the river enters Derbyshire and is joined, no doubt to its great relief, by the clear

In 1889 the Ferry Bridge over the Trent at Burton replaced the ferry that had traversed the water since the fourteenth century. Lord Burton built the bridge once the corporation had bought the ferry rights from the Marquis of Anglesey. Used as a footbridge, it is 240 feet long, has three spans and is unique of its type in Europe.

Between the City of Nottingham and the suburb of West Bridgeford the Trent has an open, almost parkland, feel at Wilford. Avenues of trees and flights of steps run down the river bank.

Boat trips operate from Shardlow and fishermen try for chub, dace, barbel, carp and roach. Towpaths are now popular walkways.

In 1947 the river swept away the Cavendish Bridge which took the A6 over the river. It was replaced, first with a Bailey bridge and then with a modern structure. The warehouses and wharves at Shardlow still remain – one of them houses a waterways exhibition – and there are narrow-boats carrying holidaymakers instead of the china clay and coal of yesteryear.

The River Trent, the Trent and Mersey Canal and the River Derwent all meet just above Shardlow and flow as one to Trentlock where they unite with the Erewash Canal, that has come down past Ilkeston and Stapleford, and the River Soar that has journeyed northwards from Leicester and Loughborough.

The Trent then has a breather from industry as it enters Nottinghamshire and passes through Attenborough Gravel Pits. Here are wintering wildfowl, terns, kingfishers and great crested grebes. Warblers enjoy the reed beds and moisture-loving wild flowers like ragged robin and yellow rattle thrive. Nearby Holme Pit is an excellent example of reed swamp with wild flowers and birds to match.

Nottingham has a long and eventful history – its castle was built by William the Conqueror in 1068 and was subsequently destroyed and rebuilt on several occasions. Richard Arkwright (see page 43) set up his first spinning machinery here in 1771, and the place

waters of the River Dove. It skirts the county town of Derby three or four miles to the south, passing under a remarkable seventeen-arch bridge dating from the thirteenth and fourteenth centuries at Swarkestone. According to legend it was built by two sisters whose lovers had been drowned trying to ford the river. For hundreds of years it was the only bridge between Burton and Nottingham.

Near Weston-on-Trent the river used to drive mills so ancient that they appeared in the Domesday Book. The power station a mile downstream now has its own option on the cooling properties of the water.

From Shardlow, just a few miles south of Nottingham, the river is navigable right up to the Humber. It has been for centuries. The Romans used it, and dug-out canoes from the Bronze Age have been found in the riverbed near Nottingham. Invading Vikings from Denmark used the river, but it was in the nineteenth and early twentieth centuries that commercial navigation was at its zenith.

Where once gravel pits disfigured the landscape, the Attenborough Nature Reserve is now a home to waterfowl. Among typha reed and willow, wild duck and geese nest and feed.

is still famous for its lacemaking as well as tobacco and bicycles.

Cascading over a weir, the river dodges around a scarp of sandstone before straightening once more and running past the tree-lined Clifton Grove on its south bank, and the works of the Boots Company to the north – Jesse Boot was one of Nottingham's greatest benefactors and later became Lord Trent.

The Nottingham and Beeston Canal nips off the river here. It was built to take craft into the heart of the city, bypassing a stretch of river that was unnavigable. It rejoins the Trent just above Trent Bridge. The Clifton Bridge carries the main road over the river at a point where generations have traversed its waters, and at Trent Bridge, the next major river crossing, is the county cricket ground. Between the two bridges ply rowing boats, sailing dinghies and mute swans.

Trent Bridge goes back to the thirteenth century, but flood and ice damage led to much rebuilding. The present bridge dates from 1871, though enlargement took place in 1925, and remains of the mediaeval bridge can be found some distance away in a garden, giving a good idea of the width of the river in those days.

It was in 1947 that Nottingham experienced its worst flooding disaster since the great flood in 1795. Half the city was awash – 2425 acres and 28 miles of street. New flood defences were the result: sluices, reinforced banks and overflow channels. As yet they have not failed.

But as well as troubling the city, the Trent has provided it with a livelihood. Henry II granted Nottingham a charter in 1155 so that its burgesses could take tolls from incoming traders. The burgesses could also fish the river, but in the late eighteenth century bathing in the river was prohibited on Sundays.

Graffiti – the scourge of the architect – scars a river bridge at Newark.

There's a Dutch feeling to the landscape north of Gainsborough where, around Owston, the land is criss-crossed by dykes.

Recreation now takes place every day of the week at Colwick, where the river leaves the city. The National Water Sports Centre shares its site with overwintering wildfowl, Canada geese, wigeon, tufted duck and pochard. The athletic flock here in summer; the avian flock here in winter.

The river meanders among green fields as it takes its leave of Nottingham. At the village of Stoke Bardolph sailing dinghies flit across the water, at Radcliffe on Trent the river bank *is* a red cliff, and at Gunthorpe is the only bridge across the Trent between Nottingham and Newark. Hoveringham Gravel Pits provide shelter for smew, goldeneye and goosander which may join overwintering wildfowl in grim weather.

The Trent runs parallel to the Roman Fosse Way, north-eastwards to

East Stoke and the site of the Battle of Stoke Field, the bloody finale of the Wars of the Roses in 1487. Four thousand men died, two years after the war was supposed to have ended. A ravine here is still known as Red Gutter.

Fiskerton is a pretty riverside village with an old mill standing on the River Greet which flows into the Trent. In the winter of 1854–5 the Trent froze over and a cricket match was played on the ice while spectators feasted on roasted sheep.

Staythorpe Power Station downstream of Fiskerton makes this unlikely nowadays, as some of the water used for cooling returns to the river warmer than when it was extracted. From here the Trent splits in two and the main course arcs around Newark-on-Trent while the rest of the water joins that of the River Devon which flows through the town itself.

Arguments over the water of this section of the Trent were rife for generations. Newark became a busy inland port in the early nineteenth century, even though in summer shallow water levels could leave boats stranded. Only in the early twentieth century did frequent dredging make the river truly navigable all the year round by providing a constant depth of 6 feet.

Newark is now a market town with the ruins of its castle towering over the River Devon. Like so many it lost its heart in the Civil War, but is still impressive when viewed from the waters below. The Trent, with the River Devon on board, leaves it to head northwards.

Between Gunness and Keadby is the only swing bridge over the Trent. It carries both road and railway and was built in 1916. Just downstream of the structure is the final power station on a river whose cooling properties have been used to the full.

Past Winthorpe Water, a former gravel pit that is now a fishery, and Holme where Dick Turpin is supposed to have watered his horse Black Bess on his way to York, the river is in snaking mood as it slews this way and that across the flat agricultural land. At Collingham remains were found of the only Roman bridge across the Trent – revealed first in 1792 in a dry summer, and subsequently lost again for a century when the fickle waters resumed their flooding.

Cromwell Lock, nearby, is the tidal limit of the river and the site of a flood control system. It is a commodious lock, capable of accommodating a fair number of boats at any one time, and there is a salmon ladder to assist the fish. Some might consider this wishful thinking on the Trent, but in 1967 two salmon were caught above Newark.

The Eagre or Hugre or Aegir, a companion for the Severn Bore (see page 132) comes up the Trent as far as the lock. This tidal wave occurs during spring high tides and can be several feet high in the lower reaches, though is much dissipated this far inland.

From Girton sand and gravel is carried on barges to Hull, and five miles to the north the river becomes the county boundary between Nottinghamshire and Lincolnshire.

Massive power stations at High Marnham, Cottam and West Burton reinforce the Trent's reputation as an industrial coolant, and Spalford marks the site of the river's greatest flooding in 1795 when the banks were breached by the torrents and 23,000 acres of Lincolnshire were submerged. It happened again in 1852, but in the last 150 years work has been undertaken to reduce the risk of its recurrence. With the Trent, nothing is certain.

Past Torksey, now a hamlet but at the time of the Domesday Book with a larger population than Nottingham, the river comes to Gainsborough. Lincolnshire and Nottinghamshire meet on this market town's eighteenth-century bridge over the Trent, and Ashcroft Mill which once stood near it inspired George Eliot's *Mill on the Floss* written in 1860.

Gainsborough is a town of historical note – King Alfred married here in 868, and King Sweyn, the father of King Canute, was murdered here in 1014. Serve him right; he had done more than his fair share of plundering. Today only Old Hall, dating from 1480, is really worth remarking on – Richard III visited it, and Henry VIII met Katharine Parr here.

Some river traffic still uses the Trent in Gainsborough, and there are warehouses and buildings that reflect the importance of the river in the town's commercial past.

North of Gainsborough, the Trent heads inexorably northwards to the sea through land that has been farmed for centuries. On its west bank is the Isle of Axholme, an area of land that has always been subject to flooding, though raised banks to the rivers and drains aim to reduce the risk of its being submerged.

Opposite Owston Ferry, Hardwick Hill rises out of Scotton Common – a wooded knoll that is the only high ground for miles – and then the Trent skirts two miles to the west of Scunthorpe, through fields as black as pitch.

A hundred and fifty years ago Scunthorpe was a tiny village. Then, in 1858, iron ore was discovered and the town mushroomed. There are steelworks here, and quarries, but the river flows on the opposite side of the town through land that has for long provided Britain with potatoes.

There are hills to the east of the river, and just 2 miles from its confluence with the Humber the river bank rises into a steep cliff that offers a superb walk along its crest. It leads to Alkborough, famous for its turf maze at Julian's Bower which is thought to have been cut by monks in the twelfth century. From the church tower in the village, on a clear day, you can see Lincoln Cathedral, Beverley Minster and York Minster, and below you are the rapids known as Trent Falls. There

Alkborough provides fine views of the river below and also boasts Julian's Bower, a turf maze reputedly cut by monks in the twelfth century.

is more than an ounce of hyperbole here. 'Falls' they are not; they are simply narrows. The Trent widened previously to around half a mile and through the constriction the water speeds up to join the Yorkshire Ouse. The two, united, change their name on marriage and become the Humber, flowing out, with everything that people have dumped in them, into the North Sea.

It would be an ignominious exit were it not for the fact that Blacktoft Sand, where the Ouse and Trent meet, is a richly populated bird reserve. So the two rivers get a send off from the reed beds and saltmarshes by bearded tits and warblers, waders such as avocets and stints, redshanks, green-shanks and, in winter, hen-harriers and merlin. The Trent deserves the acco-lade. Thanks to our industrial ambi-tions it has had a lot to put up with over the last 170 miles.

The Trent near Trent Falls where the river narrows and flows over rapids to meet the Ouse.

The Derbyshire Derwent

Height at source: 1900 feet
Length: 60 miles
Runs from Ronksley Moor to Long Eaton

In 1549... it was wild country, hard and desolate. The rocky heights behind the site of the new house carried few trees, and the River Derwent was prone to sudden and dangerous flooding. Two hundred years later, Defoe could still describe the moor you had to cross when travelling from Chesterfield or Sheffield as a 'waste and howling wilderness with neither hedge, house nor tree over which when strangers travel they are obliged to take guides or it would be next to impossible not to lose the way.

The House – A Portrait of Chatsworth by the Duchess of Devonshire, 1982

Guides are harder to come by nowadays, unless bound in cardboard covers, but the countryside at the source of the Derwent is little changed. The very sound of the name Swains Greave, up on Ronksley Moor, has a bleak ring to it, and the scenery lives up to expectations. Rough, cold and drenched in winter, with an annual rainfall of around sixty inches, this is countryside which could test waterproofs and windcheaters to the limits of their endurance.

The river rises barely five miles south of Holmfirth in Yorkshire and, after flowing northwards for almost a mile, it gradually turns east and then south to flow down through Derbyshire.

With this much water cascading down such a deep-sided moorland

Signs of a fluctuating water level can be found on the banks of the Derbyshire Derwent just before it flows into its first reservoir above the Howden Dam.

In its youth the Derwent tumbles over the rocks of the Derbyshire moorland, heading for dams that will store it to water the local population.

valley it is not surprising that seven miles further downstream is the first of four dams designed to turn the Derwent into a series of reservoirs. The story of how these reservoirs came into being reads like an account of a civil war. During the parliamentary session for 1898–9 the councils of Derby, Leicester, Sheffield and Nottingham were at loggerheads over who could legitimately lay claim to the supply. Each needed water for a rapidly expanding population. The result was

the formation of the Derwent Valley Waterboard, serving all the cities and satisfying all parties.

So it was that in 1901 construction began on the Howden Dam and a year later on the Derwent Dam.

Up on chilly Howden Moor, the men who built the dam lived with their families in Birchinlee Village, an encampment of huts that was to be their home for the next fifteen years. 'Tin Town' they called this corrugated iron settlement. There were 1000

people here, equipped with such necessities as a school, a mission room and a hospital. Now only the name survives on Ordnance Survey maps.

A railway line from Bamford provided for the transportation of the workers, and of the million and a quarter tons of gritstone needed to build the dams. Picture these men in fair weather and foul, building the Howden Dam to a length of 1080 feet and height of 117 feet, and the Derwent Dam at 114 feet high and 1110 feet long, with only primitive machinery to help them in their hauling.

During the Second World War, the long stretch of water in the Derwent Reservoir found another use, when Dr Barnes Wallis experimented with his bouncing bomb. The film of *The Dambusters* was made on location here, too.

The thirst for water continued to grow in the twenties and thirties; the Ladybower Dam, a couple of miles downstream from the Derwent Dam, was begun in 1935 and declared open by King George VI on 25 September 1945. It is the largest of the dams at a height of 140 feet and a length of 1250 feet.

The villages of Derwent and Ashopton were drowned under its waters, along with Derwent Hall, once a home of the Duke of Norfolk, the parish church of St John and St James, and assorted farmhouses.

Sinister as it sounds, this water-filled valley provides one of the most impressive car journeys in the Peak District National Park, the drive along-side the reservoirs offering views of lakes, forests and moorland. It is so popular, in fact, that a traffic management scheme is in operation at certain times of the year. Check before you set out. The scenery is grand and expansive in summer, mighty and intimidating in winter.

One dog knew that better than most. By the square and castellated towers of the Derwent Dam you will find a memorial stone to a dog called Tip. He stayed out on the moors to guard the body of his master for fifteen weeks from 12 December 1953 to 27 March 1954. Now there is loyalty for you.

The River Ashop joins the fray where it runs into the lower arm of the Ladybower Reservoir and then, at last, the River Derwent is allowed to be itself again and to flow on past Bamford.

The Derwent Reservoir has a colourful history. Created in 1902 by men whose families lived up on the moor while the dam was built, it became the testing ground for Barnes Wallis's bouncing bomb – the 'Dambuster' of the Second World War.

Once there were cotton mills on the river here, but now the chief attraction of this hill-farming village is the sheep-dog trials. These take place each year on the late spring bank holiday.

The river turns towards Hathersage, in search of literary fame. It finds it first at North Lees Hall, once the home of the Eyre family, and immortalised forever by Charlotte Brontë, whose visits to her friend Ellen Nussey at Hathersage Vicarage yielded stories of the fire that gutted a wing of the grand house. There are those who argue the case of nearby Moorseats but whatever the truth, *Jane Eyre* was most certainly born in these parts.

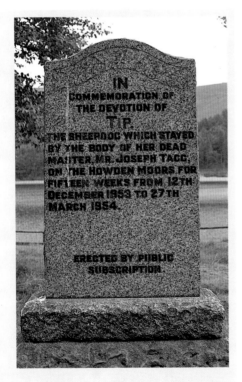

No person could have had a more devoted dog than did Joseph Tagg. This memorial to 'Tip' is beside the Derwent Dam.

With the continued demand for water the Ladybower Dam was built below the Howden and Derwent Dams and declared open by the King in 1945.

In St Michael's Parish Church at Hathersage you will find brass memorials to the original Eyre family who gave Charlotte the name for her heroine, but it is the churchyard that exerts a greater pull on those in search of legend. Here is buried Little John, the right-hand man of Robin Hood, in a grave of fitting proportions.

Little John was born in a cottage next to the church, and spent the last years of his life here. Like his pal, he fired his last arrow to mark the place of his burial. From the cottage window it flew into the churchyard and Little John followed it shortly afterwards.

Until the last century his cap and bow were hung in the church, but for some unaccountable reason were then moved to Yorkshire.

Was he large? Well, a thirty-inch thigh bone was removed from the grave in 1784 but was later stolen. The legend lives on.

Below Hathersage is Grindleford whose quarries provided the stone for the upper Derwent dams, and across the river is a handsome stone bridge. Stone predominates round here; hefty lorries chug everywhere with the stuff. The gritstone crusts of Froggatt, Curbar and Baslow Edges hang above the river valley like gigantic stone shelves. These are remnants of the Carboniferous Age erosion of earlier rivers and now provide rock climbers with a taxing training ground. Climbers of the calibre of Joe Brown and Don Whillans cut their teeth and their knees on these hunks of grit. If, like me, you prefer gentler exercise, you can enjoy the view simply by walking the tops of these edges. At the village of Calver, a Georgian cotton mill is a fine tribute to the stonemason's art. Its days as a cotton mill

long over, it was used as Colditz Castle in the television series. I dread the time when every piece of architecture in Britain is best remembered for the television series in which it featured, rather than its original use.

The water races past the mill untrammelled. Its power may no longer be utilised but the trout within its clear waters are still appreciated by anglers.

The village of Baslow, with its triangular goose green and three 'Ends' – Nether End, Over End and Bridge End – has a decent stone bridge. This no

longer needs to cope with the traffic – a new one lower down the valley has taken the strain. On the banks of the river at Bridge End is the church, with a clockface that sports the legend *Victoria 1897* instead of numerals 1 to 12. The local Dr Wrench was responsible for this, and also for the erection of the Wellington Monument which towers over the village on Baslow Edge.

It is at Nether End in the southern part of the village, that you come across the grounds of one of England's finest stately homes. Here are lodges by Wyattville, dating from 1840, which mark the entrance to the Derbyshire seat of the Dukes of Devonshire, Chatsworth House.

The Palace of the Peaks is a true rarity – a stupendous seventeenth-century feat of architecture surrounded by beautiful gardens and situated in the middle of perfect countryside. There are cascades and fountains, powered by water running through conduits from the moors. Sir Joseph Paxton, the man who designed the Crystal Palace, was responsible for much of the work here. There are woodland walks, a maze on the site of what was once the Great Conservatory, formal and informal gardens, and on the west side of the house the river glides by serenely as though it always knew it was destined to complement the landscape. The angling club fish the river here and there is an angling fair every year. The last salmon was caught in the river at Chatsworth in 1836. The fact that the course of the Derwent was diverted slightly in the eighteenth century, and

At North Lees Hall lived the Eyre family, whose name Charlotte Brontë gave to her heroine. She stayed nearby with the Nussey family.

Chatsworth House, on the banks of the Derwent – the 'Palace of the Peaks'.

James Paine's bridge was built over the Derwent at Chatsworth in 1762.

James Paine's bridge built over it, only adds to its picturesque qualities. Sheep crop the fine grass of its gently sloping banks – the scene is almost Arcadian.

Where the landscape did not quite come up to par, Lancelot 'Capability' Brown 'improved' it. Walk up the side of the Great Cascade that tumbles down towards the house and look across the valley to the river and beyond. This is Capability Brown's work at its absolute best. A succession of far-sighted Dukes have left their marks on what I reckon is the finest country estate in Britain. Even the water which cascades downhill from the moors is now being used to power turbines that provide electricity for the house.

At the south end of the Chatsworth Estate is Beeley which, like Edensor to its north-west, owes much to the work of Paxton who helped turn both into model villages without making them twee. On the moors above the river valley are bronze-age barrows and cairns.

All around there are disused lead mines, with crumbling stone huts and engine houses. They are tell-tale signs of an industry that petered out in the early part of the twentieth century.

At Rowsley, where the River Wye joins the Derwent, there are reminders that this is good trout fishing water. There is a pub called the Grouse and Claret – not a bird and a drink, but a fishing fly.

Darley Dale is the name given to the stretch of country between Rowsley and Matlock, though it is now dominated by the A6(T), robbing the river of most of its glamour. The fifteenth-century Darley Bridge at least is a reminder of how things used to be, crossing the Derwent to take traffic to Winster. To the north of the bridge are the remains of Mill Close Mine. Until closed by flooding in 1938 this was the largest and most productive lead mine in Derbyshire.

And so to Matlock. But which Matlock? There are eight of them grouped under this title, but Matlock Bath is perhaps the best known and,

along with the river, is squeezed into a steep-sided gorge between the limestone hills of Masson and Riber. There is something of the atmosphere of a Victorian resort at Matlock Bath, and here on the river in late summer are floated illuminated rafts bearing everything from the Taj Mahal to miniature paddle-steamers. There is boating here, too.

It was in 1698 that the thermal waters were discovered and the Spa established. At that time travelling to

the place was the biggest problem, but over the next two hundred years a road and railway network made things much easier. Smedley's Hydro, which dates from 1853, is now the headquarters of Derbyshire County Council.

John Smedley also built Riber Castle – a gothic schloss on the moor above Matlock. It stands roofless but robust, like a fortress with four turreted corners, visible from the valley below, and serves as a reminder of an age when wealthy industrialists could indulge their fantasies and inflict their tastes on the surrounding countryside with impunity, ruling their miniature kingdoms like feudal barons.

And yet, because of this, Matlock is a handsome town with good Victorian architecture and stupendous views, especially from the Heights of Abraham which can be reached by cable car.

It is only a mile downriver from Matlock that the greatest use was made of the Derwent as a source of power. Here at Cromford, Richard Arkwright, the father of the British cotton industry, opened the first successful water-powered cotton spinning mill in 1771. Born in Preston, this 'bag-cheeked, pot-bellied Lancashire man' made his name as a barber and wig maker in Bolton before turning to the production of cotton.

His mills still stand – at the time of writing the red-brick Masson Mill has 'To Let' signs in all its windows but the old stone mills are being restored by the Arkwright Society. At one time Old Mill worked round the clock and employed two hundred apprentices.

Matlock Bath has the feeling of a Victorian resort, crammed, like a alpine village, into a steep-sided gorge. Boats ply the river and, on Saturday evening in summer, illuminated rafts are floated on the water.

Cromford is the site of England's first successful water-powered cotton-spinning mill, opened by Richard Arkwright in 1771. It still stands and is being restored.

Arkwright was a commercial genius and boasted that he had enough funds to wipe out the national debt. Instead, he wiped out the village of Willersley – all except the mansion of Bridge House – and built Cromford near his new mill and out of sight of his new house: Willersley Castle, completed just before he died in 1792.

How things change in two centuries. Willersley Castle is now a Methodist Guest House. Had the road network, which has since changed the face of Cromford, been in existence at the time, the town might well have rivalled Manchester as the centre of the cotton trade.

For the next four or five miles the Cromford Canal runs parallel with the river, a mixture of open water and reed swamp that has become a haven for wildlife. Kingfisher, siskin and redpoll are to be found here, thanks to the encouragement of Derbyshire Wildlife Trust and Derbyshire County Council.

Among the woods on the hill to the east of the river, in the house called Lea Hurst, lived the young Florence Nightingale, while up in the hills to the west of the river, eight years after her death, lived D. H. Lawrence. In Mountain Cottage at Middleton-by-Wirksworth he watched nature in the raw. He stayed a year and in a letter to Katherine Mansfield in 1919 described the spoors of wildlife in the snow:

…little leaping marks of weasels, coming along like a necklace chain of berries; odd little filigree of the field mice; the trail of a mole…

On the slopes across the river from Whatstandwell (lovely name) and Crich Chase is Shining Cliff Wood, a Forestry Commission plantation rich in birdlife.

With woodland on both sloping banks of the river, this is one of the pleasantest stretches of the Derwent. Only at Ambergate does the work of man overpower the beauty of nature.

It is here that an eight-mile aqueduct links the Derwent with Carsington Reservoir, opened by the Queen in 1992. A vast sheet of water to the south-west of Wirksworth it contains 36 million cubic metres of water. It can be topped up by supplies pumped from the River Derwent in winter and, when the river is low, water can be pumped into it from the reservoir.

Then it is on downstream to Belper, an unashamed mill town developed by Arkwright and his partner, Jedediah Strutt, who invented the first ribbing machine for the hosiery trade and who eventually went out on his own and built seven mills at Belper. He built a mill at Makeney, too, just out of Milford. The bridge at Milford and the Makeney Mill both date from 1780.

The river takes on more water at Duffield, where the River Ecclesbourne joins it, and now the City of Derby is barely a couple of miles away. Once Darley Abbey was a separate village, ruled over by the Evans family who lived in the Hall and built the cotton mill. Now it is part of the city itself.

You would think that through a city a river would take a back seat. In Derby things are different for Derby has Project Riverlife, a scheme intent on restoring and conserving flora and fauna and all manner of riparian organisms.

This is no easy task, especially when dealing with a city river that is not intrinsically a thing of beauty, thanks to the industrial activities on its banks. But the relative lack of pollution in the Derwent, and the shallowness which makes it un-navigable, have resulted in it being a haven for wildlife. Kingfishers in the centre of town, damsel flies flitting over the water and the presence of freshwater crayfish are proof of the water's purity.

But the river can be wild and moody, too. Water draining off the surrounding clay soil makes the river rise rapidly after heavy rain – which is why the arches of the bridges across the Derwent in Derby are higher than you would expect.

The shallow edges of the river support a richly varied flora, from branched bur-reed to monkey flower and figwort. On the banks are Indian balsam with its exploding seedpods (a rampant foreigner that needs to be kept in check), meadowsweet, hemp agrimony, welted thistle and the ubiquitous willow herb.

It is when the river is low and slow-moving that you stand the best chance of seeing a kingfisher dive from a partly submerged branch or stake for its prey. The nests are in tunnels bored into the soft river banks. Finches and warblers cavort among the alders and willow,

Belper still has some of the appearance of a mill town – from the towering red brick edifice of North Mill by the main road, to the bridge and weir. At one time the weir at Belper powered eleven wheels.

goldfinches tease the seeds from thistle heads, and on the surface of the water glide pochard, tufted duck, mallard and mute swans, though, until the banning of lead fishing weights, lead poisoning took its toll of the swans.

The fishermen are after perch, roach, gudgeon, chub, dace and pike which swim here, along with the occasional river lamprey – an eel-like fish which attaches itself to other fish as a parasite.

Youngsters go for the minnows and sticklebacks in the shallows.

There are numerous nature reserves along the Derwent in Derby, including one on the water intake lakes of the Courtaulds Factory to the south-east of the town where over 120 species of birds have been spotted. There are several open days at this reserve during the year. A little upstream is Alvaston Park, where Canada geese, moorhen, coot and swans congregate. Few English towns can boast of such a breadth of birdlife.

Derby has a modest place in history. The district of Little Chester is where the Roman fort of Derventis was established, and Derby Bridge marks the southernmost point of Bonny Prince

Far from taking a back seat, the Derwent in Derby is now a focal point for pleasure and leisure.

It was Jedediah Strutt who built the double weir on the Derwent at Milford to power his mills. Even today it is regarded as a remarkable piece of construction work. Strutt's engineering was always more ambitious than that of Richard Arkwright and his factories, sited by the weir, were better equipped.

Charlie's advance in his quest for the throne in 1745. He failed, and did not try again.

On the river near All Saints Church was built the first English mill in 1717 – Lombe's Silk Mill. Jedediah Strutt built a mill here, too. He and his son William, who built the first iron-framed mill which finally reduced the ever-present fire risk, are buried in Derby Cathedral.

Derby is a city famous for its railway, and for the fact that Henry Royce chose to build his car factory here. Even today Derby is workmanlike rather than architecturally grand.

The river leaves the town at its south-east corner and snakes its way in serpentine curves towards Long Eaton. Past Draycott and over weirs at Church Wilne, it slides forlorn and forgotten into the cold, wide, grey-brown Trent in the shadow of the M1.

The Great Ouse

Height at source: 500 feet
Length: 156 miles
Runs from Brackley to King's Lynn

Slow-winding through the level plain
Of spacious meads, with cattle sprinkled o'er.

from *The Task* by William Cowper, 1784

The Great Ouse is a fenland river and, writing in 1909, A.G. Bradley reckoned it 'the most characteristic of East Anglian rivers, as it is unquestionably the most important of them.' But it starts life on the borders of Oxfordshire, Buckinghamshire and Northamptonshire, as a brook in a shallow valley, and at this early age it acts as the county boundary between the three.

It is a river that will see tremendous changes in scenery before it flows into the Wash. Nowhere is the landscape dramatically hilly, but the gently rolling countryside of its youth – the grassy banks that drip with gnarled old willows – will eventually be replaced by flat and windswept fens that use the river as a drain.

The Upper Ouse is a restless river. Its course is fidgety and wriggling, and like a liquid worm it slithers past the outskirts of Brackley where, in a castle that has now vanished, the negotiations for Magna Carta took place in 1215. Trout can be fished in this stretch of the Ouse Valley, but the fish decline to swim any further downstream once the river reaches a town it slices clean in two – Buckingham.

Decreed the county town in 886 by King Alfred, it lost the honour to Aylesbury in 1725 after a great fire had destroyed much of its grandeur. By today's standards the town is still handsome, with a market place and streets that climb the hillside. It was once an important wool town, until its inaccessibility brought about its demise, but the market place still has its cattle pens. Catherine of Aragon rested here as Queen in 1513, and Charles I held a council of war in

One water course crosses another at Cosgrove, north of Milton Keynes, where an iron aqueduct carries the Grand Union Canal above the Great Ouse.

Castle House a century later. Nowadays there is a pleasant riverside walk in the town, and the Great Ouse exits on the eastern side to flow past the Old Mill House. It is swelled by the waters of Padbury Brook – the first of many tributaries that reinforce the Great Ouse's reputation as a shifter of water.

From historic Buckingham the river heads north-east towards a town with, as yet, no history at all: Milton Keynes.

I remember advertisements for this new town, perhaps twenty years ago, showing a bucolic scene of fishermen lounging on the river bank amid rampant greenery, limpid water and benevolent trees. The slogan was something on the lines of 'Wouldn't you rather be in Milton Keynes?' The river wouldn't. It skirts the town to the north, but it does offer fishermen roach, chub, bream, barbel, dace,

Many gravel pits that once scarred the countryside are now flooded to create nature reserves. These Canada geese are part of a rich collection of waterfowl and insects at the ARC Wildfowl Centre in Buckinghamshire.

gudgeon, stone loach and spined loach; the population varies depending on the depth and speed of the water. Pike, ruffe and perch can be found where the river slows its pace.

At Cosgrove, to the north-west of the town, the Great Ouse passes under the Grand Union Canal and is then joined by the River Tove. United, the two flow past the water skiers cavorting on the old gravel pit. A mile further downstream the river snakes between a chain of twelve flooded pits that provide coarse fishing for anglers and fascination for avid bird watchers. One of these artificial lakes is the ARC Wildfowl Centre, where a plenitude of waders and waterfowl paddle and swim, especially in winter. Described as the best bird reserve in Buckinghamshire, the centre is open to groups by appointment. So successful are dragonflies at breeding on the lake and the river that SSSI status has been given to the area, and hobbies approve, too, swooping in to take their share of food on the wing. Summer visitors include travelling ospreys and bitterns, and Cetti's warbler has also been spotted here.

This stretch of the river is clear and clean – pure enough to support grayling. After playing tag with Newport Pagnell at the top right-hand corner of Milton Keynes, the Great Ouse takes the River Ouzel or Lovat with it and turns northward to begin its long journey to the Wash.

After six miles the Great Ouse comes to Olney, famous as the home of the poet William Cowper. The 185-foot spire of the Church of St Peter and St Paul dominates the landscape and stands right by the river. It is a fourteenth-century church, and in 1767 its vicar of the time, the Revd

The Great Ouse flows through many villages including Great Barford to the north of Willington.

'The Cage' at Eaton Socon, built in 1826 for the confinement of local malefactors.

John Newton, persuaded William Cowper and his companion Mrs Unwin to come and live here. The calming influence exerted by the widow Unwin over the emotionally unstable Cowper was all but undone by the 'gloomy piety' of the reverend gentleman, but together the cleric and the poet penned what came to be known as the 'Olney Hymns', including 'God moves in a mysterious way His wonders to perform', 'How sweet the name of Jesus sounds', and 'Glorious things of thee are spoken'. In the Market Square the house where Cowper and Mary Unwin lived is now a museum. Later they moved to the 'The Lodge' in the nearby village of Weston Underwood and that, too, still stands.

Cowper died in 1800 and is commemorated by a window in the church at Olney. He fails to escape the Revd Newton even in death – the two are pictured together, with a hare.

With slightly less speed than a hare, the river continues northwards and for the next fifteen miles it is at its prettiest. Canoeists who are happy to tipple over the weirs between Olney and Bedford can see the Great Ouse at its best. The picturesque village of Turvey was rebuilt of local stone in the nineteenth century to become a sort of Victorian model village. 'Delectable and ornate' A.G. Bradley called it at the turn of the century, and it still is.

The adjacent villages of Harrold and Odell now have a joint country park where dragonflies thrive and the number of water birds is building up. Smew, goldeneye and red-necked grebe are prominent in winter, Canada and greylag geese, along with mallard, are there all year round. Warblers enjoy the reed beds and the willow wands. Further downstream at Felmersham is another bird population – all of them utilising what once were gravel pits.

The Great Ouse is great at changing its mind, and having flowed northwards for some miles it now decides on a southerly course, looping to east and to west alternately, past disused mills and 'osier holts' and an assortment of villages with such names as Sharnbrook, Milton Ernest and Pavenham. At Stevington is a fully restored windmill, and at Bromham the mill by the river was built in 1695 and now runs again as part of an exhibition on milling. The surrounding water-meadows are rich in wildlife but picnickers can enjoy them, too. Eventually the river passes Kempsford and reaches Bedford, flowing through the county town from west to east. Riverside walks along the Great Ouse at Bedford are encouraged. The long island called Mill Meadows surrounds a boating lake, and boats can also be hired on the river.

Bedford is famous as the home of John Bunyan (1628–88), the 'Immortal

Tinker', who was born at Elstow, a mile to the south of the town. A spirited youth, he turned to God after marrying and raising a family, but sought a simpler form of worship than that of the established Church. He would preach on village greens around the town and was eventually imprisoned for his non-conformist beliefs in the County Gaol at Bedford. He used the time to write his best-seller, *The Pilgrim's Progress*, published in 1678. Bunyan lived in a house in the town (as well as spending twelve years in its gaol) and plaques mark the site of both. There is also a statue of Bunyan on St Peter's Green, and a museum at the Bunyan Meeting Church holds much of interest, including the celebrated window of Bunyan writing his *magnum opus*.

As the river leaves the town, streams flow through watermeadows to join it, decorated by willows and alders and anglers. The village of Willington, just outside Bedford, marks the upstream navigational limit for the Danes who built harbours and docks here. Twenty-five longships could put in at any one time and the shape of the docks can still be seen. It is amazing to think that these vast boats had a draught of only 3 feet.

In the seventeenth century the river was commercially navigable as far upstream as Bedford – a facility eventually removed by silting up, the difficulty in maintaining constant water levels, and the construction of numerous mills and weirs. The coming of the railway further reduced commercial river traffic. Nowadays the river is still navigable to pleasure craft between Bedford and the Denver Sluice at Downham Market, though water levels vary with the season and the National Rivers Authority's information sheets are essential reading.

Farmers of the area have long valued the river's nourishing effect on the land. William Gooch, writing in 1811, said: 'Its quality is such that in six weeks it will fatten a bullock or a horse though put into it bone lean.'

Ducks take to the water at St Neots, a town that owes its name to the Benedictine priory which stood here in the tenth century.

At Godmanchester the Chinese Bridge of 1827 carries pedestrians to an island on the Great Ouse.

St James's Church at Hemingford Grey – is its spire at the bottom of the river?

meadow of fritillaries, yellow rattle, ladies bedstraw and meadowsweet, here is a floral delight through which the nuns used to stroll on their way to Hinchingbrooke on the outskirts of the town. The river runs around the meadow from which hay is still taken each July, and then it flows eastwards to the south of Huntingdon and St Ives, and to the north of Godmanchester and Hemingford Grey.

All four places have their own fascination. Huntingdon was the birthplace of Oliver Cromwell in 1599 (Hinchingbrooke was the family seat of the Cromwells, though Oliver never inherited it). Godmanchester was a Roman settlement. Hemingford Grey is a picture-book village of thatched cottages – the spire of its riverside church, which blew off in a gale in 1741, is said still to be at the bottom of the river. St Ives (known until 1050 as Slepe) changed its name when a priory dedicated to St Ivo was built there.

A small quay still stands on the river at St Ives, serving as a reminder that this was once an important port for barges from northern Europe. The handsome stone bridge over the river is fifteenth century and possesses one of only four surviving mediaeval bridge chapels in England.

None of the three mill wheels remains at Houghton Mill, between Huntingdon and St Ives, but much of the equipment in this seventeenth-century mill is still on view. It is administered by the National Trust. There has been a mill on this site since 969, and the present mill was still

It is through such agricultural countryside that the Great Ouse is now destined to flow. Turning northwards once more it is joined by the River Ivel and passes assorted villages until it arrives at Eaton Socon. Here stayed Charles Dickens, in the Old Plough Inn, and he mentions the village in *Nicholas Nickleby*. Pepys came here, too, when Eaton Socon was a coaching town. Now it is a part of the adjacent St Neots, a market town named after the Benedictine Priory that stood here in the tenth century. The market square is on the river bank and the Bridge Hotel by the river dates from 1685. You can

walk the Great Ouse from here to Earith – a total of 26 miles – on the Ouse Valley Way.

North of St Neots is Little Paxton, whose water-filled gravel pits, adjacent to the river, are described as being the most interesting of those in the Ouse Valley. Here are to be found masses of wintering wildfowl and passage waders. There is a heronry, a tern colony, and warblers and nightingales enjoy the reed beds and willow scrub. It is a place of amazing riches.

So is Port Holme Meadow, on the edge of the river's next port of call, Huntingdon. An ancient 300-acre

The waters of the Great Ouse at Houghton Mill have powered mill wheels for over a thousand years.

grinding corn in the early part of the twentieth century. It was something to which the Great Ouse was well suited. The Domesday Book lists twenty-three mills on the river and its tributaries in Huntingdonshire alone. Am I alone in pining for their return?

Downstream at Holywell is the thatched Old Ferry Boat Inn which has been selling ale since 1068. Here, in the bar-room floor, you can see the gravestone of poor Juliet Tewsley who hanged herself on a riverside tree on 17 March 1050; the woodcutter Thomas Zoul spurned her attentions on his way home from work, in spite of the fact that she offered him a bunch of flowers. Her ghost is said to appear each St Patrick's Day.

Through farming country the Great Ouse flows northwards to Earith which, from the river's point of view, is the gateway to the Fens. Its route from now on has been totally dictated by

Ye Olde Ferry Boat Inn at Holywell has been selling ale to the locals since 1068.

man. In mediaeval times the river took a more westerly route from Earith, joining the River Nene and eventually flowing into the Wash under the name of Welle Creek at Wisbech (Ouse Beach). It was crossing Welle Creek, and not the Wash, that King John lost the Crown Jewels.

Today the Great Ouse runs farther to the east, and at Earith there run from it what look like two vast canals. These straight-as-a-die channels of the Old Bedford River and the New Bedford River (or Hundred Foot Drain) cut directly towards the coast to meet up with the Great Ouse again at the Denver Sluice near Downham Market.

The Fens produce such an amount of water that the river, once tampered with, was incapable of coping with it. The two parallel channels, excavated to drain the adjacent fens into a central reservoir and to take the water more speedily to the sea at King's Lynn, date

from the seventeenth century – the Old Bedford River from 1630 and the New from 1649, when the Earl of Bedford brought in the Dutch architect, Sir Cornelius Vermuyden. Now the twenty-mile-long piece of marshy fenland they enclose is a nature reserve known as the Ouse Washes.

Managed by the Royal Society for the Protection of Birds, the Cambridgeshire Wildlife Trust and the Wildfowl Trust, these washes are literally awash, not only with water but also with wildfowl. There are 30,000 wigeon, swans (including ten per cent of the world's Bewick swans) and waders which breed here in spring. There are snipe and black-tailed godwits, hen harriers, shovellers, and many more species. The northern end is the Wildfowl Trust's Welney Reserve.

Many thousands of years ago the Fens were woodland, and lumps of unidentified tree, always referred to as 'bog oak', regularly come up from the peat during ploughing. The build-up of peat is thought to have killed off the trees, and the flooding that followed, perhaps coupled with subsidence, again affected the nature of the land. Some islands rose above the low-lying areas, and on these were built towns and villages. Hence the Isle of Ely (Eel Island) which the Great Ouse passes on its current route, to the west of the two Bedford Rivers.

Ely Cathedral is a stunner. Begun in 1083 on the same site as a seventh-century Benedictine Abbey, it can be seen and sighed over for miles around. The tower collapsed in 1322 and was replaced by a superb octagonal lantern.

At Earith water spills out over the Ouse Washes.

Ely Cathedral has dominated the fenland countryside since it was built in 1083. It occupies the site of an abbey founded in 673 by St Etheldreda.

imprisoned. Never again did the Bishops of Ely wield such power.

Fishing in the plentiful channels of north-west Norfolk can produce bream, roach, rudd, pike and zander. The last-named is a predatory fish capable of very fast growth and blamed by some for the greatly depleted stocks of other fish in the water courses. Could the zander, introduced from Holland, be solely responsible, or is fertiliser leaching partially to blame?

With few bends the river runs northwards for fifteen miles now, taking on the Little Ouse at Brandon Creek and eventually reaching the Denver Sluice. This gigantic moveable dam is symbolic of the centuries-old disputes surrounding the Great Ouse, and the differences in opinion between those who would use it as a navigational channel and those who regard it as no more than an elaborate land drain. The 'Fen Tigers' destroyed the

Boats and ducks busy themselves on the waterfront of the Great Ouse at Ely.

Walk from the cathedral down to Cherry Hill Park, on the banks of the river, and take a look at the rest of Ely. It is now a predominantly Georgian market town but Henry VIII founded King's School.

Through flat and hedgeless fields as black as soot and past vegetables in serried ranks, the river, tightly corseted by its banks and marshalled into a straight line, is joined by the River Lark and flows past Littleport, famous for its riots of 1816. Local farm-workers rebelled because the food they had grown and needed to survive was being shipped out to London to swell the coffers of their farming landlords. They marched on Ely, and then returned home. At the behest of the Bishop of Ely eighty men were subsequently arrested: five were hanged, five were deported and the rest were

The present-day tranquility of Littleport belies its turbulent past. In 1816 the local farmworkers rebelled and marched on Ely claiming rights to the food they were growing. Arrests, hangings, deportations and imprisonment followed.

first sluice built by Vermuyden in 1652. These eel catchers and wild-fowlers did not want the Fens drained, and neither did sailors and merchants. But replacement sluices were built, and now a tight control is kept here over tidal flow to ensure the safety of England's market garden.

The story of the draining of the Fens is a complex and fascinating one. It is a tale of slow ebb-tides exacer-bating the silting up, of horses and carts destroying unstable river banks, of constant alterations to the river's course, complex engineering and disas-

trous flooding. At Denver these factors come to a head, as do all the strands of the Great Ouse and the Bedford Rivers – seven channels in all, including the enormous Cut-off Channel which snakes its way through the surrounding Norfolk countryside.

Opened by the Duke of Edinburgh in 1964, this channel starts near Mildenhall in Suffolk, to the east of the Great Ouse, and prevents water from the rest of Norfolk and Suffolk from draining into the Ouse or finding its way to the Fens. Tributaries can be diverted into the channel when neces-

sary, and the system will hopefully prevent any repetition of the great flood of 1947 when the Great Ouse burst its banks. Seventy thousand acres of the Fens were flooded and Ely became an island again.

Such worries about flood and destruction are soothed at Denver by the sight of yacht masts that rise above the sluice gates. This is the home of the Denver Sailing Club, and the vast network of artificial waterways is now plied by narrow boats as well as sailing dinghies. Where once cattle, sheep and vegetables were shipped across the countryside, people now enjoy the trip instead. From Denver to Huntingdon will take you seven days; you will need a fortnight to make it to Bedford. Upwell is the place to hire narrow boats, which can be navigated from the River Nene to the Great Ouse via Well Creek at Salter's Lode.

So, having taken on the water of numerous tributaries and drains, the Great Ouse, swollen as much as its engineers dare allow, flows past Downham Market with the Riley Channel beside it. This great canal carries the water of the Cut-off Channel, and both it and the railway have come between Downham Market and the river, robbing the town of its original role as a great river port.

Now the river passes through marshlands as distinct from fens. Marshlands are nearer the sea than fenlands and on slightly higher ground. As a result they have buildings from earlier times, and the villages of Wiggenhall St Mary Magdalen,

There are four Wiggenhalls in the Norfolk Marshlands. At Wiggenhall St Peter the ruined church stands right on a bank of the Great Ouse.

Bell, is a delight. Four square and pinnacled it is a reminder of Lynn's past: merchants have traded here since mediaeval times, as buildings like the Hanseatic Warehouse of 1428 testify.

The port is still a thriving concern, with docks that handle everything from Skoda cars to timber, grain, fertilisers, steel and fuel. The fishing fleet is one of the few that have expanded in recent years due to an increased demand for shellfish, and there are plans to build a new river berth.

The Great Ouse, heavy with water, is joined by the River Nar at King's Lynn, and flows out into the Wash. I half expect it to sigh with relief.

Wiggenhall St Peter, Wiggenhall St Mary the Virgin and Wiggenhall St Germans are worth exploring for their churches and their inns. Eels are caught on the river here and, for those who relish them, smelts.

Between the villages of St Mary and St Germans is the biggest pumping station in England, lifting water from the Middle Level Main Drain into the Great Ouse. From here the river flows to Kings Lynn.

'Lynn', as the locals call it, is a fine market town (Tuesdays and Saturdays), in spite of the fact that parts of it are now blighted by the same plastic fascias that muck up many an English street. But there is also a generous legacy of great architecture, much of it connected with the river. Merchants' warehouses still run down to the Great Ouse and the Custom House, built as a merchants' exchange in 1683 by Henry

King's Lynn, with its Custom House built as a merchants' exchange in 1683.

The Wensum

Height at source: 160 feet
Length: 30 miles
Runs from Whissonsett or East Rudham to Norwich

Very flat, Norfolk.

Noel Coward in *Private Lives*, 1930

Mr Coward obviously went to a different part of Norfolk; the Wensum flows through a landscape of woods and meadows that is gently rolling. The young river is a picturesque sight with only one drawback from my point of view – that of locating its source.

Take Mr and Mrs Miller who live at Shereford. They are closely acquainted with the Wensum as it flows through their garden. But ask them where the source is to be found and Mr Miller points in one direction and says Whissonsett, and Mrs Miller points in another and says East Rudham. The locals have argued over it for years. I am nervous of taking sides, so I have to tell you that from East Rudham the River Wensum flows eastwards to Tatterford, or from Whissonsett it flows northwards to Tatterford past Raynham Park, home of Viscount Townshend – a descendant of 'Turnip' Townshend who wrote *Horse Hoeing Husbandry* and who pioneered crop rotation. From Tatterford both parties are in agreement and I think I am on safer ground.

The market town of Fakenham lies to the north of the River Wensum. It's a pleasant, if modest, town with a mixture of architecture and a church that dates back, in part, to the fifteenth century.

The Upper Wensum is a clear stream that gurgles through rich green pastures: if Kent is the 'Garden of England' then Norfolk must be the meadow. You could be forgiven for thinking that this was an ordinary and unassuming little river; it is only 10 feet wide at this point and trundles along quite harmlessly. But for much of its length the Wensum is designated a Site of Special Scientific Interest. The upper reaches are fed by springs that rise from the chalk and also by run-off from nutrient-rich soils, so the riparian vegetation is lush and invertebrates thrive.

Further downstream, boulder clay and river gravel overlie the chalk to provide a greater variety of habitat, and mill weirs and sluices further enrich the diversity of river life. On the river bank much of the land is grazed or cropped for hay and, being low-lying, it is subject to flooding. All these factors combine to make the Wensum a treasure trove for naturalists.

Around Shereford and Sculthorpe the water supports freshwater crayfish (though it is said many of them are illicitly removed to supply Chinese restaurants), and brown trout is the dominant species of fish. The middle and lower stretches of river are frequented by chub, pike, roach, eel and barbel. Kingfishers and little grebes feed and breed along the river, and the reed beds are alive with reed and sedge warblers. It is also one of the few parts of the country with a healthy barn owl population.

Expanding modestly in size, the river heads eastwards to pass through Fakenham – a pleasing, if unremarkable, town with up-and-down streets, a market square and a few Georgian houses. Many of the houses in these parts are of brick and flint, the roadside verges are wide and awash with cow parsley in spring, and the cows themselves look up at you as you pass. The much-praised Pensthorpe Waterfowl Park and Nature Reserve occupies flooded gravel pits on the outskirts of the town, and at Great Ryburgh the Church of St Andrew has, like many churches in Norfolk, a round flint tower dating from Saxon times (there

The Wensum is naturally rich in wildlife but its riches are added to when it skirts Pensthorpe Waterfowl Park where exotic birds rub shoulders with the natives.

The church at Little Ryburgh is now a ruin, but in the churchyard a white marble angel hovers over the Smith family vault – a landmark visible from afar.

were no cornerstones to be found in this part of the country).

The next stretch of water – between Guist and Norwich – is well populated by otters. The river-bank habitats suit them, and so does the fish population.

At Bintree Mill I was greeted by the owner who showed me inside the ancient building that has been in his family since 1880. The mill wheel was smashed up before the war, but water-powered turbines ground pig-meal and the like until the 1970s. Now the building is empty and the river unharnessed, but the owner catches eels in the Wensum by stringing his long cylinders of nets across the water inlet in August and September when the eels are running. His family swim in the mill pool, and a rowing boat floats among the flag irises. He would not give it up, he says; it has been in the

Sawyers Mill at Lenwade, like most mills in England, no longer harnesses the water. Nearby gravel pits are regularly fished.

family too long. He earns a living from farming and letting out the mill to the odd film company. Having given me a whistle-stop tour he went back to filling in his land set-aside forms.

A disused railway track runs alongside this stretch of the river, and a road sign points you in the direction of County School Station. The school has long since gone, but the station, a train

and a short length of track remain – lost in a time warp. Ah, but wait. County School Station will be the northern terminus for $17\frac{1}{2}$ miles of track from Wymondham one day.

There is little activity now at the ruins of the Saxon Cathedral at North Elmham. This was the seat of the Bishops of Norfolk from about AD 680 until the late eleventh century when it

moved to Thetford and then Norwich. From here the river turns eastwards through meadowland, past flooded gravel pits and disused mills, a wildlife park at Great Witchingham (Lenwade), and eventually snakes down through Taverham and Drayton to its grand finale in the city of Norwich.

The Wensum is the river at the heart of the city, while the Yare caresses

The 315-foot spire of Norwich Cathedral, from the quiet of the Cathedral Close.

The Bishop Bridge across the Wensum is the only mediaeval bridge left in Norwich.

its southern boundary to meet up with the Wensum on its exit. Mousehold Heath is a hill that rises above the city and from here you can count the towers of its churches – at least twenty of them soar above the houses. The greatest is that of Norwich Cathedral, topped by a spire, at 315 feet. The view was beloved of the Norwich School of painters, among them John Sell Cotman and John Crome.

As cities go Norwich is among England's finest. Parts of the city wall and its gates remain, as do mediaeval buildings and alleyways, and the Norman keep of Norwich Castle. The awe-inspiring cathedral dates from 1096.

The river is entwined with industry – Norwich is famous for shoes, for mustard and for printing. This book is itself a product of Jarrold Publishing while Jarrold Printing uses the water of the Wensum to cool its presses. Both companies are housed in what was formerly a Victorian yarn mill on one bank of the river.

The Wensum acted as part of the city's fortifications in the early days, and then helped it to become the second city of England for many years. Stone from France was carried upstream to build the cathedral and, until the 1980s, cargoes and coasters still made their way into this inland port. Now the River Wensum swaggers through the town, past the French Empire railway station where it fills the yacht basin, and then heads south to join the River Yare. It was such a modest stream just thirty miles ago; excitement came to it late in life.

The Yare

Height at source: 250 feet
Length: 50 miles
Runs from Shipdham and Whinburgh to Great Yarmouth

. . . I was quite tired, and very glad when we saw Yarmouth. It looked rather spongy and soppy, I thought, as I carried my eye over the great dull waste that lay across the river; and I could not help wondering, if the world really were as round as my geography book said, how any part of it came to be so flat.

from *The Personal History and Experience of David Copperfield* by
Charles Dickens, 1850

The mill that straddles the Yare near Bawburgh was once home to Jeremiah Colman, great uncle to Jeremiah James Colman, famed for his mustard.

If it is not Noel Coward remarking on Norfolk's lack of contours it is Charles Dickens. Still, during the final miles of the River Yare (pronounced Yair) they are both justified. At its source the landscape has more the feeling of gentle downland as the chalk springs emerge from Norfolk meadows. Eventually they join to become the Yare and snake eastwards between Brandon Parva and Barnham Broom, whose mill buildings straddle the river. Trout, grayling and coarse fish populate the water, finding shelter among the weed that thrives here in summer.

The River Tiffey flows into the Yare at Barford, and four miles further downstream is a hamlet which, at one time, rivalled Walsingham as a place of pilgrimage. Bawburgh was the burial place of St Walston, a prince turned farm labourer. When Walston was buried in 1016 a spring began to flow from the ground and the place thereafter became a shrine. The hamlet nestles in a shallow valley and from the three-arched bridge across the river you can look upstream to the old mill that once belonged to Jeremiah Colman, who moved to Norwich in 1804, and whose family were to make a fortune out of something most people left on the side of their plate: mustard.

From Bawburgh the river wriggles north and south until it reaches the City of Norwich. While the Wensum flows through the city, the Yare cradles it to the south, gliding through the grounds of Earlham Hall, since the early 1960s the site of the University of East Anglia.

The Yare has a long tradition as a rowing river, pre-dating the University Boat Race between Oxford and Cambridge. The Carrow Cup, struck in 1813, is still rowed for today, between Norwich and Whitlingham three miles downstream. There are several rowing clubs in the city as well as a regatta.

It is at Trowse, on the edge of Norwich, that the Wensum flows into the Yare, and from here the river enters that stretch of countryside known as the Norfolk Broads. To enjoy the Broads, most boaters choose the River Bure to the north. But there are broads on the Yare, too. The first is Surlingham Broad, reached by passing through Thorpe (once called the 'Richmond of Norfolk'), and the picturesque scenery of Bramerton Woods.

The Broads owe their origins to the digging of peat in mediaeval times. On average they are five to six feet deep and skirted by reeds and flag irises.

Alders and willows grow in 'carrs' where rotting vegetation has consolidated to make damp earth over the years. The popularity of 200 miles of water linking around thirty Broads has resulted in their being watched over carefully by the Broads Authority so that erosion, excessive reed growth, pollution and agriculture can be controlled to ensure their survival.

While the motor cruiser carries most people over the Broadland waters today, it is the wherry – a clinker-built boat – that is the classic Broads craft. All manner of cargoes were carried by these oak vessels, from reeds and timber to coal and chalk. With a mast far forward so that it could be lowered easily to pass under bridges, the wherry had a large hold and a cabin to

The riverside at Thorpe where the 'Old River' is used for pleasure traffic. A new cut was dug in 1844 so that commercial traffic could by-pass two low railway bridges on this section of the Yare.

Walks around Strumpshaw Fen promise rich encounters for wildlife enthusiasts.

Strumpshaw Fen where the Royal Society for the Protection of Birds' nature reserve has been isolated from the River Yare to protect it from pollution.

provide accommodation for a skipper and mate, the normal crew.

The last wherry was built in 1912, and by 1949 not one of them plied its trade on the Broads. The few that survive do so thanks to enthusiasts and the Norfolk Wherry Trust. Along with the decoying of wildfowl, the wherry has become a piece of history. How long before eel catching and the cutting of reeds for thatch join them?

At least the river and its adjacent Broads and vegetation are a refuge for wildlife. The RSPB's reserve at Surlingham has open water, marshes and reed beds where many warblers breed and bats flit around at dusk. At Strumpshaw Fen, another reserve downstream, the RSPB has avoided the risk of pollution that exists on the Yare below Norwich by isolating the marshland from the river. Over-enrichment by nutrients from agriculture and treated sewage effluent can cause a build-up of algae that has a harmful effect on other water life. It is a problem that is being addressed by the Broads Authority and the NRA in a major research project.

At Strumpshaw these dangers are by-passed. The plant known as water soldier has a valuable colony, and marsh harriers and the Norfolk aeshna dragonfly co-exist. The Yare valley is the British stronghold for Cetti's warbler and hosts the only flock of bean geese in England. But then this whole area is a naturalist's paradise.

The Norfolk reed beds are home to bitterns, great crested grebes, bearded tits and swallowtail butterflies. The bitterns boom over the water as the Yare snakes through marshy ground past Brundall, a good centre for pleasure boating, and on to Cantley, scented by a sugar beet factory, and Reedham. A chain ferry at Reedham is still the only crossing point on the Yare between Norwich and Yarmouth.

It is to Yarmouth that the Yare now journeys. It is added to by the River Chet at Hardley Cross and the River Waveney is artificially joined to it by New Cut at Reedham. Through fields bisected by ditches and pumped dry by windpumps, many of which today stand bereft of sails, the Yare writhes through the now flat countryside.

The river really ends when it flows into Breydon Water, a vast estuary which in Roman times made Reedham a great sea port. This large sheet of tidal water, and its mudflats, is a valuable overwintering site for waders and wildfowl, now administered by the RSPB and the local and county councils. Posts mark the navigation channel through the estuary; the unwary beach themselves on the mudflats.

It is almost an anti-climax from here when the estuary narrows again to pass under a modern road bridge, but at least the town of Great Yarmouth, or Yaremouth, turns to face the river. Here the Yare is joined by the Bure before it glides through a three-mile-long channel that sandwiches a long finger of the town between river and sea. There are still signs of its mediaeval and Victorian past, though it was badly bombed during the Second World War.

Once the home of a busy herring fleet, Yarmouth today makes a living from tourism and business brought its way by North Sea Gas. To the south of the town the Yare bursts out into the North Sea at Gorleston, along with gas industry supply vessels and assorted shipping. Twin beacons wink as it takes its leave.

'The last working vehicle ferry in East Anglia', claim the operators of the Reedham Ferry. It remains the only way of crossing the Yare by car between Norwich and Yarmouth. The Reedham Ferry Inn provides Dutch courage.

A great herring fishing port for over a thousand years, Great Yarmouth now relies on tourism and the North Sea Gas industry. Some of its ancient town wall and mediaeval narrow alleys, known as 'rows', survived war-time bombings.

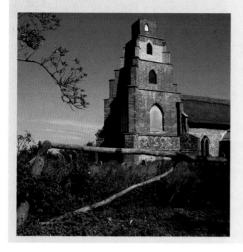

The Waveney

Height at source: 100 feet
Length: 50 miles
Runs from Redgrave to Breydon Water
The otter is far wilder than the fox . . . the otter has no home except the river and the rocky fastnesses beside it. No creature could be more absolutely wild, depending solely on his own exertions for existence.

from *The Life of the Fields* by Richard Jefferies, 1884

In squelchy fens between Redgrave and South Lopham the Little Ouse and the Waveney rise back to back, one either side of the B1113, and then flow in opposite directions – the Little Ouse eastwards to Thetford and the Waveney westwards to Diss.

Some rivers start their life quietly, sneaking into being with a gentle trickle in country backwaters. The Waveney is allowed only two miles of obscurity before it comes upon Bressingham Gardens and Steam Museum, where gleaming locomotives hiss and toot their salute as they clank along its banks. Alan Bloom is the man whose passion for steam has enlivened Bressingham.

The Waveney is different in character from those nearby rivers, the Yare and the Wensum, which have their origins in chalk springs. Pollution is a problem and although the river is much cleaner than it was, run-off from intensive agricultural holdings can still impair its quality. It is a sluggish river, and chub, roach and dace are the Waveney's main fish.

Right from its source the river acts as the boundary between Norfolk and Suffolk. Flowing to the south of the market town of Diss through green pastures and agricultural land dotted with clumps of trees, it makes slow progress; water runs in from ditches and drains and the river makes a loop to the south of Harleston. There is plenty of Georgian architecture in Harleston and two market places. Across the river is Mendham, the birthplace of Sir Alfred Munnings, one-time President of the Royal Academy, most famous for his paintings of horses. He was the son of the local miller, and the

Reflecting the twin passions of one man – Alan Bloom – steam engines and border perennials give the Waveney a colourful and noisy send-off at Bressingham, near Diss.

The Otter Trust at Earsham has done much to preserve this sleek mammal.

countryside around the river still tempts many to set up their easels.

Five miles downriver is the place that has done most to reinstate the otter on British rivers: The Otter Trust at Earsham, near Bungay, run by Philip and Jeanne Wayre. Since 1983 they have released over forty otters into the wild, and in most areas the animals have increased in numbers with no further introductions. In its upper reaches the Waveney has a good population of otters. Around Earsham and further downstream the land is more open with meadows and marshes, and they appear only sporadically.

Past the honking wildfowl on the lakes at the Otter Trust it is only a mile before the river encircles Bungay, a town greatly damaged by fire in 1688. Georgian houses reflect the town's prosperity as a river port in the eighteenth century.

Wriggling through marshland the river passes through its tidal limit at Geldeston Lock and approaches the town of Beccles. Where once commercial river traffic plied the waters, the space is now given over to pleasure craft, and the 92-foot bell tower of St Michaels' Church is a focal point.

From here it is only ten miles to the coast at Lowestoft, and that might be where you would expect the Waveney to head. Instead, it cuts a great arc around Burgh St Peter whose thatched church is on the river bank. A mile downstream, Oulton Broad is connected to the Waveney by a dyke.

Snaking northwards now, the Waveney passes Somerleyton Hall and gardens, and the only complete smock windpump surviving in Norfolk – Herringfleet Marsh Mill.

At St Olaves there is another windpump and now the river finally loses it job as the boundary between Norfolk and Suffolk. St Olaves is the site of an Augustinian priory whose ruins have been restored, and nearby is Fritton Lake and Country Park. But it is also the point at which New Cut, a drainage and navigational channel excavated in the eighteenth century, links the Waveney across country with the Yare. Boats are plentiful.

The scenery changes dramatically here, the landscape flattening as the river proper heads out over the marshes past Belton and Burgh Castle to flow into Breydon Water. It drifts into the great estuary alongside the Yare, to be carried with it into the North Sea at Great Yarmouth.

The thatched church at Burgh St Peter has a tower of gradually diminishing cubes.

The Thames

Height at source: 360 feet
Length: 210 miles
Runs from Thames Head at Coates to Southend-on-Sea

Never in his life had he seen a river before – this sleek, sinuous, full-bodied animal, chasing and chuckling, gripping things with a gurgle and leaving them with a laugh, to fling itself on fresh playmates that shook themselves free, and were caught and held again. All was a-shake and a-shiver – glints and gleams and sparkles, rustle and swirl, chatter and bubble. The Mole was bewitched, entranced, fascinated.

from *The Wind in the Willows* by Kenneth Grahame, 1908

Good old Moley! Of pure enough mind not to be worried by abstraction, pollution, erosion and vandalism, and capable of seeing the river for all its delights. It was the Thames at Cookham Dean that inspired Kenneth Grahame to write his best-seller, and in the river's upper reaches – far away from Parliament and flood barriers, Wandsworth and Wapping, and the eventual maritime pleasures of Southend-on-Sea where flags in sand-castles wave it goodbye – it is still a handsome country river.

The source of the Thames is marked by a slab of stone under a towering ash tree, but of water there is no sign. This is at Trewsbury Mead between the villages of Coates and Kemble in Gloucestershire, marked Thames Head on the Ordnance Survey map.

These are the lower slopes of the limestone Cotswolds, with Cirencester

Ashton Keynes in the Cotswolds where the young river Thames slides lazily by daffodil bedecked banks and cottages of honey-coloured stone.

barely three miles away. Mind you, some folk claim that the true source of the Thames is at Seven Springs, three miles south of Cheltenham. I am sticking with the Thames Head route.

If John o'Groats to Lands End seems too long, then set yourself the task of walking the Thames Path, due to be completed in 1994. It follows the river for 180 miles from the source to the Flood Barrier at Woolwich; Duncan Mackay's *The Secret Thames*, published by Ebury Press in association with the Countryside Commission, makes an excellent guide.

River banks are home to a wide variety of birds, including wagtails. The grey wagtail usually makes its nest near fast-running streams but in winter can be found near slower waters.

The Thames takes its name from the Sanskrit *tamas*, meaning 'dark', thanks to its waters which are often dark and cloudy. At the point marked as the source, a puddle would be cause for celebration. When the infant river does eventually appear in a field near Kemble, its whereabouts are celebrated with a mattress of moisture-loving, bright yellow kingcups.

It has somehow made its way from the source and trickled underneath the old Fosse Way – once a Roman road and now the A433. It is between the A433 and the A429 that you can first see the stream.

The nipper of a river dawdles past the villages of Kemble and Ewen. Except when swollen by surface water, the river is clear in its upper reaches, reserving its darkness for adolescence.

'River Thames or Isis' it says on the map as the river makes for Somerford Keynes. Coots honk among the marshy stream margins as the water runs by the old Cotswold manor house and south of the village before passing through Neigh Bridge Country Park on its way to Ashton Keynes. Here the river is shunted firmly into second place as it meekly makes it way between vast sheets of water that were once gravel workings. The land becomes a patchwork of lagoons, and to the north of the picturesque village of Ashton Keynes, replete with honeyed stone cottages and half a dozen bridges that cross the little river, the artificial lake district rejoices under the enticing name of the Cotswold Water Park.

Flooded gravel pits, through which the Thames winds near Ashton Keynes, are known as the Cotswold Water Park – good for water sports and bird life.

In these lime-rich lakes invertebrates and fish thrive, and flitting between them are marsh and grasshopper warblers and ringed plovers. Garganey and great crested grebe paddle the water and the secretive water rail makes its home in the reedy margins.

It is within the next three miles that the river undergoes a rapid adolescence. Other tributaries join it, including the unappetisingly named Swill Brook, and at Cricklade the River Churn flows in.

Before it reaches the town, the river passes through one of the most important nature reserves in Britain. Here, at Nar Mead, or North Meadow, grow millions of snakeshead fritillaries, making up eighty per cent of the total number in Britain. Between March and April the meadow is awash with white and dusky purple chequered bells. Adder's tongue, meadow rue and southern marsh orchid follow.

The Lammas land here is a relic of England's ancient meadow land; haymaking in July with subsequent grazing and winter flooding make it ideal for the growth of the snakeshead and other rarities such as yellow rattle.

Cricklade marks the end of upstream navigation rights on the Thames, though most boats can get no further than Lechlade, some ten miles downstream. It was always an important crossing point, being the border post between the Saxon kingdoms of Mercia and Wessex, and during the nineteenth century a plank bridge across the river was used for baptisms.

In the churchyard at Lechlade, Percy Bysshe Shelley wrote 'Stanzas in a Summer Evening Churchyard', having rowed up the Thames from Windsor with Thomas Love Peacock, Mary Godwin and Charles Clairmont in 1815. They failed to reach the source of the Thames so stayed overnight and rowed back the next day.

No splash on the forehead here but baptism by total immersion.

The stronger river now passes through farming country to Kempsford, within earshot of RAF Fairford to the north. The church here was built by John of Gaunt in 1390 and around it are the meadows that supported the sheep that gave a livelihood to the farmers from mediaeval times onwards. The river watered the meadows, washed and fulled the wool (shrinking and compacting it) and was the life-supporting artery of the communities in these parts.

Having flowed to the east for several miles, it now turns northwards to Inglesham where it is enriched by its marriage to the River Coln – crystal trout-filled waters that now disgorge their riches into the Thames. At the confluence of the rivers is Inglesham Round House, once a lock-keeper's cottage on the Thames and Severn

Canal. This was the waterway designed to take traffic from east to west of the country, when roads could not cope with heavy commerce.

Inglesham is the grand entrance to the canal from the Thames, which brought cargo from London on its way to the Severn Estuary. Traffic in the opposite direction included salt from Droitwich, fruit from Evesham, coal from Staffordshire and copper from Swansea. A stupendous feat of engi-neering, with forty-three locks along its 28 miles and the Sapperton Tunnel at 3817 yards (2.2 miles) long, it was opened in 1789. But when the railway network made its mark in the nine-teenth century, it dwindled into retire-ment and was abandoned in 1927. Now there are fragments of it between here and Stroud, enjoying a secondary life as pocket nature reserves, and a third of the Sapperton Tunnel has been opened up for boat trips.

The river says goodbye to the Costwolds at Lechlade, the point at which upstream navigation ends for all craft with anything but the shallowest draught. The 'Gateway to the Cotswolds' is a Georgian market town, a 'lade' or loading point where Double Gloucester cheeses began their journey downriver. The uppermost lock on the Thames, and the uppermost boatyard, are here, as the numerous and varied pleasure craft testify.

The barge trade made the town of Lechlade prosperous, but Half-penny Bridge also endeavoured to add to the coffers. In 1839 there was a revolt which resulted in the ha'penny toll for travellers on foot being withdrawn. The toll-house still stands at the town end of the bridge – a reminder of times when the power of the pedestrian was greater than it is today.

The statue of Old Father Thames by Rafaelle Monti now reclines by St John's Bridge.

Campbell, an Australian, built a distillery by the riverside to make alcohol from sugar beet. The stuff was shipped downriver and thence to France for brandy production but the scheme did not last long. Today the house is renowned for its art collection and the estate for its model farm.

If you are searching for idyllic spots on the Thames, Kelmscott, just across the river from Buscot, is hard to beat. The home of artist and scholar William Morris from 1871, Kelmscott Manor is a sixteenth-century Cotswold stone house. It is now a museum but only open on rare occasions.

At Radcot, to the east of Kelmscott, is the site of the oldest bridge across

Between Lechlade and Teddington Lock, on the outskirts of London, anglers can land bream, perch, pike, chub, gudgeon and roach, and above Lechlade brown trout are abundant. Barbel and tench are hooked on occasion, too, as well as dace and bleak. A mile downstream at St John's Bridge, the River Leach, which gives the town the other half of its name, joins the Thames, as does the River Cole. This is a lovely spot, where the stone road bridge makes use of the central island in the river for support, and has an arch over each of the two channels of water to allow river traffic to pass underneath. There are locks and this is also the final resting place of Rafaelle Monti's statue of Old Father Thames.

The river tumbles over Buscot Weir and flows past the National Trust's Buscot Estate where, in 1879, Robert

The pumps in Buscot village are accommodated in grand style.

the Thames. There is supposed to have been a bridge here since 958, and the central arch of the present old bridge is rounded rather than pointed like the other two, thanks to alterations made by Henry Bolingbroke (the future Henry IV) in 1388. A newer bridge now takes the traffic. From the wharf here, stone from local quarries was taken downstream for the building of St Paul's Cathedral.

The scenery now is agricultural right up to the river bank, with only the immediate margins providing a haven for wildlife. The river divides at Radcot Bridge, the northern fork being navigable and the southern fork heading for Duxford, where the ford is in a blissful setting among willow trees.

This is Oxfordshire, and the River Thames or Isis is heading for the county town. The River Windrush joins it at Newbridge. At Bablock Hythe the Physic Well was once a popular spot; now it languishes among bushes, little more than a murky trickle. The river flows northwards past Stanton Harcourt, where the church and the manor house, in whose tower Alexander Pope turned Homer's *Iliad*

into verse, sit calmly by a stew pond once bursting with carp. At Swinford the bridge still extracts a trifling toll.

Then the river turns south for Oxford and its dreaming spires. From the ivy-swamped Trout Inn at Godstow, a twelfth-century hostelry that was once a hospice for the nunnery on the opposite bank, students punt down through Port Meadow to the Perch, a thatched pub at Binsey. This piece of country positively reeks with history. Henry II's mistress, the Fair Rosamund, spent her last years in the nunnery (now a riverbank ruin). Lewis Carroll dreamt up *Alice in Wonderland* on a boat trip from Binsey to Godstow on 4 July 1862, reciting it to the young Alice Liddell as the family boated through Port Meadow. This ancient common land is protected from any kind of cultivation except the grazing of cattle, horses and geese. Rare flowers grow on the river bank – among them tubular water dropwort and great burnet – and birds and wildfowl find refuge here, too. When the river floods and freezes it mirrors the spires of the town.

Christchurch Cathedral looks towards the river across its own meadow, and at Folly Bridge, just upstream, you can hire punts. No one knows just where on the river the ox-ford was, nor why the river has always been called the Isis at this point, but Oxford is somewhere to linger and explore. I do not have time or space and must move on with the Thames.

It meets up with the Cherwell, Oxford's famous punting river, before leaving the town, gliding through

Henry Bolingbroke, the future King Henry IV, removed the central arch of Radcot Bridge to foil supporters of his brother who were fleeing south – and it shows.

Folly Bridge, across the Thames at Oxford, is named after the one-time gatehouse lived in by Sir Francis Bacon.

meadows of fritillaries and reeds, through Iffley Lock and the stretch of water used by the Oxford Colleges for their rowing. There are 'Torpids' in February, and 'Summer Eights' in June – real regatta days.

Past Nuneham House, a Palladian residence set in Nuneham Park, with grounds by 'Capability' Brown, the river cuts an arc westwards now to Abingdon, and stays to this side of the town, dividing to make Andersey Island. The town lies one side of the

river, fields and woodland the other.

Past Culham, and through Sutton Pools at Sutton Courtenay, the river turns eastwards again to the pretty village of Clifton Hampden. The Church of St Michael and All Angels sits on a knoll above the river, and the mellow brick bridge was designed by Sir George Gilbert Scott on his shirt cuff and built between 1864 and 1867. It is a simpler affair than his other creation, the Albert Memorial, built five years later.

The Barley Mow, by the bridge, gets an honourable mention in Jerome K. Jerome's *Three Men in a Boat*: he is reputed to have written a few chapters here, which is probably why he felt honour bound to say that it was 'the quaintest, most old-world inn up the river', and that in 1889.

From Clifton Hampden the river cuts another arc in a clockwise direction to the historic Roman town of Dorchester. This is the other Dorchester (not the one of Thomas

Hardy) and it is presided over by an Iron Age hill fort and Wittenham Clumps, both on the Sinodun Hills, an ancient Celtic site.

The River Thame joins the Thames here, and the latter drops its pseudonym of Isis. A jigsaw of water-filled gravel pits surrounds the town, and in the moist ground alongside the rivers grow coppiced willows.

It was in the River Thame that King Cynegils of Wessex was baptised by St Birinus in 635 and Christianity was brought to much of southern England. The nearby village of Berinsfield takes its name from him.

Southwards now through Shillingford and Benson, famous for its RAF base, towards Wallingford, and what I always think of as that string of Ox-Berks-and-Bucks towns on the Thames. Here moored pleasure boats show that, in spite of the bustle of the town, some folk have their priorities right.

Wallingford was an important river-crossing for the Romans, the Saxons, the Danes and the Normans. Today it is a market town with fine Georgian houses and a seventeenth-century pillared town hall. A handsome bridge, thirteenth century in part, crosses the river.

Six miles downstream are the twin towns of Goring and Streatley. At Streatley, to the west of the river, the ancient Ridgeway meets the Thames – the one an important route on land in ancient times and the other a prime means of water transport.

Between Goring and Maidenhead the river meanders past wooded chalk hills where beech trees cast down their

The Celts occupied high ground on the Sinodun Hills at Wittenham Clumps. From here there are stunning views of the valley of the Thames below, across to Dorchester with its Norman Abbey.

arching branches and meadows flank the waters. In the woods behind Streatley, during the 1930s, the BBC recorded the song of a nightingale. Do its offspring still sing here?

More exotic vocalising can be heard by the river at Lower Basildon in Childe Beale Wildlife Park – a patchwork of ponds, pools and pastures where rare animals and birds can be found. As nature reserves go this one is especially attractive.

Whitchurch-on-Thames comes next, then Pangbourne, where Kenneth

Grahame spent his last years in Church Cottage. This is the stretch of river visited by Ernest H. Shepherd to make his drawings for *The Wind in the Willows*, and Jerome K. Jerome describes it as 'glorious'. His three men put in at the Swan by the weir at Pangbourne and ended their journey, sadly, in pouring rain.

But no setting could be more glorious than that of Mapledurham House, a couple of miles downstream from Pangbourne, which really can boast 'Queen Elizabeth I slept here'. It

Fine stained glass, including that of the Jesse window, can be found in Dorchester Abbey.

is a warm brick house of manorial proportions dating from 1588 and is still lived in by the Blount family who built it. Surely this was the inspiration for Toad Hall? Its mill (see page 78) still grinds corn – the only working mill on the Thames.

From the river's point-of-view Reading has little to recommend it. A busy town with much traffic, it is easy to forget that Henry I lies buried here in the remains of a Norman abbey. The Thames passes between the suburb of Caversham to the north and Reading to the south, and then turns northwards to Sonning and a renewal of those home counties' pleasures of boating and fishing and detached houses with gardens running down to the river.

The gardens of the Deanery at Sonning are worth a look – designed by Gertrude Jekyll to complement Edwin Lutyens' house built for the editor of *Country Life*. At Sonning is the last road bridge over the Thames before Henley. It is a handsome eighteenth-century eleven-arched, red-brick structure, cradled by willow trees. The old water mill at Sonning is now a theatre.

The River Loddon flows into the Thames at Wargrave (row against its current and you are supposed to feel sick!). There are boatyards here and an annual regatta. The village has a green at its centre and, at the time of writing, the owner of Wargrave Manor is the Sultan of Oman.

Shiplake, between Wargrave and Henley, owes the derivation of its name to sheep lake – the lake was once used for sheep dipping. Alfred, Lord

One look at the Thames near Goring and you can see why it has been designated an area of outstanding natural beauty. This chalk valley has the Chilterns to the east and the North Wessex Downs to the west.

Tennyson married Emily Sellwood here in 1850, which was also the year he became Poet Laureate.

And then the river reaches Henley-on-Thames, home of the Royal Regatta each July. Once so elitist that no tradesmen were allowed to compete, the annual junket now attracts rowing crews from schools all over Britain, and spectators who occasionally manage to see a race between tent poles and awnings and an alcoholic haze, thanks either to copious amounts of Pimm's or of Brakspear Ale, the town's own brew.

The week before the Regatta all swans are removed from this stretch of the Thames, and put back the week after. The man charged with this task is John Turk of Cookham, who for thirty years has been the Queen's Swan Keeper, following in the steps of his father who held the post for forty-one years. It is John who supervises the annual tradition of 'Swan Upping', carried out each year during the third week in July.

All the swans on the river belong to either the Queen or to one of two City Livery Companies: The Dyers' Company and the Vintners' Company. During Swan Upping week the Queen's Swan Keeper in his randan – a traditional Thames craft propelled by three rowers – is accompanied by skiffs carrying the City Livery crews. Their job is to identify the ownership of the new crop of cygnets by examining the bills of the parents. Swans belonging to the Dyers' Company are given one 'nick' in the side of the bill, and those of the Vintners' Company have a 'nick' on either side. The Sovereign's swans are unmarked. If the mating pair belong to different owners the progeny are divided.

The voyage in the boats begins at Sunbury on a Monday, and works its way up river for a week, ending at Dorchester on Friday. The men make a fine sight: the Queen's Swan Keeper in his scarlet jacket, white trousers and naval cap, and his men in their scarlet jerseys. The Vintners are dressed in bottle green and white, and the Dyers in dark blue and white. Regaled in their finery they pen the swans against the bank with their six boats, then proceed to examine the parents and mark the cygnets. John Turk admits that there are occasions when these gaily caparisoned men end up in the water.

With one stop for lunch at a local hostelry the party moves on towards their next group of birds. Since the banning of lead weights for fishing on the Thames several years ago, John Turk has noticed a marked increase in swan numbers – now up into the hundreds. With each swan living for fifteen to twenty years, the future of the birds that Richard the Lionheart is reputed to have introduced to Britain from Cyprus seems secure.

The Thames around Henley can be enjoyed at all times of year for its walks to Marsh Lock upstream and for boating past Temple Island. Fawley Court, upstream of Henley, was built by Sir Christopher Wren in 1684 and has grounds laid out by 'Capability' Brown.

Then the river turns east to Hambledon Mill, which was in use until 1957, and passes through Hambledon Lock near Remenham – something of a bottleneck during regatta week.

There are forty-three locks between Lechlade and Teddington, each designed to maintain water levels in the navigable stretches of the river. But they also provide a most pleasing diversion for spectators from the river bank, watching barges and ship's captains of varying expertise working off their lunch.

We go westerly with the water to Medmenham now, the site of an old ferry used by Charles II in 1678, and Medmenham Abbey (see page 80). You would not guess from its dignified exterior that this was once the home of Sir Francis Dashwood's Hellfire Club. In the mid-eighteenth century Dashwood leased the Abbey and it became the setting for all manner of scandalous goings on. Satanic rites were enacted in the shrubbery and the gentry cavorted around in monk's habits chasing scantily clad nymphettes through the Abbey ruins. How different from the nobility of today.

At Hurley there is a weir, a marina and a multitude of eyots (pronounced 'aits') – little islands furnished with willows. A new footbridge crosses the river at Temple; it was specially built in 1989 to carry the Thames Path over the water.

Pillboxes were built on the banks of the Thames in 1940 to protect the river in the event of an invasion. They were never used.

The path has a good view across the river to Bisham Abbey, founded by the Knights Templar in the twelfth century. It was the only monastery which Henry VIII restored after the dissolution and became part of the divorce settlement of Anne of Cleves. Elizabeth I slept here, too, but the building is now the National Sports Centre run by the Sports Council.

Bisham Church is right by the water – an idyllic spot for this handsome church with a Norman tower. Inside is a memorial to Lady Elizabeth Hoby, lady of the manor, a scholar who beat her son to death for blotting his copy-book. Evidently a lady with a short fuse. Behind the church are Quarry Bank Woods, now owned and managed by the Woodland Trust. This stunning beech wood was badly damaged by the two great storms in 1987 and 1990 but with replanting it will regain its former glory. It is the 'Wild Wood' of *The Wind in the Willows*, home to the weasels, stoats and other 'wild wooders'.

A mile downstream is Marlow. Once an important river port, this is a handsome town with its famous pub, the Compleat Angler, on the river bank. The Compleat Angler is a smart hotel now, with little of the charm it had in Izaak Walton's day 350 years ago. Then it had only six rooms; now it has sixty. The willow tree in the garden is reputed to have been planted by the Duke of Wellington. The town is an unlikely place to have spawned *Frankenstein* but it was here, in Albion House, that Mary Shelley, wife of the poet, wrote her thriller.

On the opposite bank to Marlow lies Cookham Dean where Kenneth Grahame spent much of his childhood, and where he lived with his wife and son between 1906 and 1910. *The Wind in the Willows* was published in 1908.

Cookham's other famous resident was the artist Sir Stanley Spencer, whose work is now exhibited in a converted Methodist chapel. His most famous work, 'The Last Supper', is in Cookham Church. Cookham has been an important place on the map for centuries. There are Bronze Age barrows here and two huge lumps of stone: Cookham Stone and the Tarry Stone, showing activities of earlier civilisations. The river was an important crossing point for the Romans.

Cookham Dean, Cookham Rise and Cookham itself are almost encircled by the river as it turns south towards Maidenhead, and by the bridge is the boathouse of John Turk, the Queen's Swan Keeper. The river divides and creates islands here, before reuniting

The mill at Mapledurham, between Pangbourne and Reading, has reputedly ground corn since before the Norman Conquest and was probably doing so when Moley and Ratty had their picnic beside it in Wind in the Willows. *It is still an idyllic spot, swathed in swags of willow by a bank bedecked with daisies.*

and flowing past Cliveden, which is set high up on the east side above a wooded bank. It was once the home of Nancy Astor, Britain's first woman Member of Parliament, and the gathering place of the Cliveden Set, a sort of Hellfire Club without the fire. Now the house and grounds are the property of the National Trust, but the house itself has been leased to a company who run it as an exclusive hotel.

Alongside Maidenhead the river runs through Boulter's Lock, managed in Edwardian times by one W. H. Turner, assisted by Juggins, his bull terrier. It was a famous spot then, through which passed pleasure steamers crammed with gents in boaters and ladies with parasols; today

The bridge at Henley-on-Thames with its masks of Mother Isis looking upstream and Father Thames looking downstream. The swans have to be removed for the duration of the regatta.

Remenham churchyard where the gravestone of the nineteenth-century lock-keeper, Caleb Gould, declares: 'The world's a jest and all things show it, I thought so once and now I know it.'

it is another of those 'giggling spots' where you can pass an idle hour watching amateur boaters nudging one-another through the lock gates.

Maidenhythe was the town's name in the thirteenth century, and it is now a place of grand houses with gardens sweeping down to private moorings. The bridge built across the river for the Great Western Railway by Isambard Kingdom Brunel in 1838 still ranks as the world's longest single-span brick-built bridge. InterCity 125s race across it today.

The river swings eastwards now past Bray, and Michel Roux's famous Waterside Inn, through Dorney Reach within sight of the splendid Tudor house of Dorney Court, immaculately preserved in its sixteenth-century splendour. It was here that the first pineapple was grown in Britain and presented to Charles II.

Monkey Island Hotel, in the centre of the Thames, was used in the film *Hope and Glory*. It is a quaint place with timbered verandahs, decorated with paintings of monkeys in sporting

As you glide by peaceful Medmenham Abbey in a boat it is difficult to believe that this was once the venue for Sir Francis Dashwood's Hellfire Club. Here, in the eighteenth century, all manner of naughty goings-on took place in the shrubbery. Nymphs were chased through the Abbey ruins by men dressed in masks. Tut tut!

Windsor, at the end of the Chilterns, it gets a good send-off by the landmark that has been home to the British monarch for centuries.

The water skirts the mound of the castle, first begun by William the Conqueror and added to by forty kings and queens of England. From the Round Tower twelve counties are visible. There are 4800 acres of great park in which the descendants of William's deer still roam, and the castle itself is the largest lived-in castle in the world. The fire of 1992, which destroyed St George's Hall and other state rooms, stunned the nation. It also led, directly or indirectly, to the Monarch agreeing to pay income tax. The prospect of public coffers having to foot the bill for the damage brought things to a head.

The prospect of having to foot the bill for a child at Eton College would bring things to a head in most households, too. Strange to think that the world's most famous public school was founded in 1440 to educate two dozen poor boys. Since then it has schooled crowned heads and twenty future prime ministers. The Chapel stands out among the school buildings, surrounded by playing fields which, said Noel Coward, had made the owners of the stately homes of England 'frightfully brave'. They row on the river, too. You can cross it by footbridge from Eton to Windsor or wander down Eton's High Street trying hard not to stare at the boys in their tailcoats and Eton collars.

The Thames makes an 'S' bend

poses. The Duke of Marlborough was responsible for their being painted in 1744, though the island really takes its name from Monk's Eyot, a one-time monastic cell. Now conditions are far from monastic, and in the grounds of the hotel peacocks, ducks and geese flaunt their feathers. Strange to think that the island was made from debris dumped here from the Great Fire of London in 1666.

Through farming and market gardening country the river now meanders towards nobility and regality. The nobility are found at Eton, and the royals at Windsor.

Windsor Castle marks the end of my favourite part of the Thames, of the real river, complemented rather than swamped by people. From here on, the water is hemmed in by housing and industrial premises but at least at around Windsor, past the village of Datchet and underneath two bridges built under the direction of the Prince Regent. One, the 'Albert Bridge', replaces a ludicrous structure built by Berkshire and Buckinghamshire councils – one half in timber, the other half in iron. The bickering councils ended up with a bridge with differently designed halves and with one half three inches lower than the other. It stood for forty years before its demolition.

The low-lying flood plain between here and Walton-on-Thames suffered greatly in March 1947 when a series of Atlantic depressions brought heavy rain. Coupled with mild weather which melted the snows upriver, torrents of water flooded the land. *The Times* of 19 March reported that below Chertsey Bridge the Thames was three miles wide; a mile wide at Walton. Wraysbury, Datchet and Runnymede were cut off. The water was six feet deep in places, including Maidenhead. It was the worst flooding since 1894 and has not been equalled since.

The bridge over the Thames at Marlow runs right by All Saints Church and is the only surviving bridge designed by William Tierney Clark who also constructed a bridge across the Danube. It offers fine views of the river.

Today the most regular pain in the neck is the roar of aircraft. They thunder down to Heathrow over the Queen's country seat and over nearby Old Windsor where Edward the Confessor had his wooden palace which was spurned by William the Conqueror. Archaeologists found the remains of a Saxon mill here, with three wheels, glazed windows and a mill leat (a narrow channel for bringing water to the mill wheel) an amazing 1200 yards long. It was the only Saxon mill found on the river and was destroyed in the early tenth century.

It is round the next bend in the river that the second most memorable date in English history is celebrated. If 1066 and the Battle of Hastings is the most memorable, then 1215 and Magna Carta must come next. At Runnymede, King John is reputed to have signed the document which ceded to the demands of his barons; the field now also boasts a memorial to President John Fitzgerald Kennedy and one to those men of the air force who lost their lives in the Second World War – all 20,455 of them.

A glance at the Ordnance Survey map now reveals the river snaking its way between assorted sheets of water. These are reservoirs and filled-in gravel pits on the Thames Valley Flood Plain that have become home to wildfowl such as grebe, pochard and tufted duck. It passes through Staines, a town which nobody would now call attractive, though it was once an important river-crossing for Celts and Romans. Before locks were made further down-stream, this was the limit of the Thames tidal flow.

The river makes an ox-bow at Penton Hook, coming right back on itself, and there are marinas and little boats moored at the bottom of bunga-lowed gardens around the island in the middle. Then it flows through Laleham by Laleham Abbey, past Chertsey, the site of an abbey in 666 (now untrace-able), through classy Weybridge, Walton-on-Thames and Sunbury-on-Thames, past weirs and locks and eyots to Hampton where the actor David Garrick's temple sits on the side of the river, just across the road from his villa.

On Tagg's Island here, in the 1800s, Fred Karno had his 'Karsino', where Laurel and Hardy and Charlie Chaplin later performed. In addition the island now boasts smart houseboats, whose owners seem a world away from the gypsies who cut the long-vanished beds of osier. Huck's boathouse is a strange sight: a Swiss chalet perched between road and river, but the next building on the Thames must surely be its grandest – Hampton Court Palace.

Begun in 1514 by Cardinal Wolsey, Hampton Court Palace became the

At Runnymede is the Magna Carta Memorial erected by the American Bar Association in 1957: 'To commemorate Magna Carta, symbol of freedom under law.' What of the English Bar Association?

favourite country home of Henry VIII. Here he lived with five of his wives – two of them (Jane Seymour and Catherine Howard) are said still to haunt the place.

The wondrous astronomical clock in Clock Court was designed by Nicholas Oursian in 1540 and among the information it gives is the time of high water at London Bridge. The roots of the famous greenhouse-grown grapevine, planted at Hampton Court in 1768, are said to draw sustenance from the river which skirts the park to the south before heading northwards through Kingston upon Thames. This was the crowning place of Anglo-Saxon kings, as the Coronation Stone near the Guildhall testifies.

Then to Teddington and the first or last lock on the Thames (the lock downstream at Richmond is only used when the flood barrier is in position). In the drought of 1976 the river flowed backwards here, pumped upstream by water engineers to allow abstraction for public consumption at Molesey. When, in normal circumstances, the water is allowed to flow over it, the weir at Teddington is the most spectacular on the river.

In the centre of the Thames at Twickenham is Eel Pie Island, once a tree-covered eyot that was popular for picnics. Here Morleena Kenwigs, in Charles Dickens' *Nicholas Nickleby*, came 'to make merry upon a cold collation, bottled beer, shrub and shrimps, and to dance in the open air to the music of a locomotive band.' No mention of eel pie, though it was made

The palace that is arguably England's finest – Hampton Court. So grand that Cardinal Wolsey felt obliged to give it to King Henry VIII.

in these parts at one time from a delicious-sounding mixture of eels, sherry, shallots, butter and lemon all wrapped up in pastry.

Past Ham House, the seventeenth-century home of the Duke of Lauderdale, the river passes through Richmond, and from the top of Richmond Hill is the best view of the mature Thames. J.M.W. Turner, Vincent Van Gogh and Sir Joshua Reynolds all painted the view of the sinuous silver ribbon below. The area was so like his Yorkshire earldom of Richmond that Henry VII rechristened it; up till then it had been known as Sheen, a name still applied to the area between Richmond Park and Barnes. The park itself, replete with deer, is 2400 acres in extent and an oasis for Londoners intent on an instant day in the country.

Past Old Deer Park, the river runs by the Royal Botanic Gardens, Kew, my early training ground and home to Decimus Burton's Palm House, William Chambers' Pagoda and the brand new Princess of Wales Conservatory. Kew is the finest botanic garden in the world – over 200 acres packed with fascinating plants. Started in 1759 by Princess Augusta, the mother of George III, it became a home for 'Farmer George' for part of his life. It was opened to the public in 1840 and remains, to this day, a combination of botanical research institution and public delight. Kew Palace, the smallest of the royal palaces, is open, too.

On the opposite bank of the river is Syon House, home to the Dukes of Northumberland, situated midway between Isleworth and Brentford. With

Kew on one side and Syon House on the other, the great brown Thames slides by, now living up to its cloudy name. It looks as if it could offer little to wildlife other than an untimely death. But the river is much cleaner than it was a hundred years ago when the stench was overpowering and the water devoid of life. Today, thanks to the efforts of the Thames Water Authority, there are far fewer pollutants in its murky depths, and a surprising number of fish can be found even in the London stretch.

Salmon were plentiful in the river during the eighteenth century, with sixty a day being taken at Maidenhead in 1804. By 1830 they were gone, and it was not until the 1960s that the water became clean enough to risk re-introducing them to a Cotswold stream which would eventually feed the river. The first salmon was taken by rod on the river in 1983, and now all catches must be reported and recorded. Eggs and fry are being placed in the upper tributaries, and anything between one

Kew Gardens sits on the banks of the Thames. Decimus Burton's Palm House, completed in 1848 at a cost of £30,000, has recently been restored at far greater cost.

There are pike in the River Thames and at last the general fish population is building up again thanks to improved controls over pollution.

hundred and five hundred salmon make their own way up the river each year from the sea. Sea trout are also being seen with increasing frequency, in addition to the river's other residents: eel, roach, dace, bream, bleak, carp, bullhead, stickleback, rainbow trout, common goby, pike, rudd, perch, flounder and smelt.

Below Kew Bridge the river changes in aspect and, although the banks in places still bear trees and grass, the overall look is harder and greyer in preparation for London proper.

Pleasure cruisers chug upriver to Kew and Hampton Court from Tower Pier, and through Barnes, Mortlake and Putney you can see rowing crews being bawled out by their coaches who cycle perilously along the towpath with loud hailers. Each year in March is the University Boat Race when Oxford and Cambridge compete on this chilly stretch of river, followed by a small armada of motor launches, while spectators cheer from the towpaths on either side.

When the tide goes out great, grey-green, greasy mud banks appear, to be picked over by gulls and waders. The turning of adjacent Barn Elms waterworks into a nature reserve will provide a habitat for even more.

Through Chiswick, Hammersmith, Fulham and Chelsea on its north banks, and Barnes, Putney, Wandsworth and Battersea to the south, the river passes under a series of bridges that can become a family game as you try to name them in the right order:

Battersea, Albert, Chelsea, Grosvenor (railway), Vauxhall, Lambeth, Westminster, Hungerford (railway and foot), Waterloo, Blackfriars, Southwark, Cannon Street Railway Bridge, London (rebuilt) and Tower Bridge.

In Battersea Park, alongside the river, there are rare delights. Once a rather seedy spot, it was converted into a riverside park in Victorian times and occupied by the Festival of Britain funfair in 1951. Now it is the unlikely site of a wildlife park and nature reserve where eighty-eight species of birds, 143 different wild flowers, eleven dragonflies and twenty-four butterflies can make their home.

On the opposite bank is Cheyne Walk, Chelsea, with plaque after plaque recalling the famous residents

Strand-on-the-Green, just downriver from Kew Bridge, has handsome cottages on the river bank and a popular pub called the City Barge.

Living on the river bank is all very well in fair weather, but when the wind gets behind the tide at Strand-on-the-Green, flood protection is advisable.

of this select river frontage: J.M.W. Turner, Hilaire Belloc, George Eliot, Whistler, Brunel and Rosetti. There are houseboats, too, ranks of them rising and falling with the tidal waters.

From here on down, the Thames is rich in metropolitan history. It seems that almost every building on its banks has a tale to tell, from the Tate Gallery to Lambeth Palace, from the Houses of Parliament to the South Bank's Royal Festival Hall and the Royal National Theatre. Their stories have been told elsewhere. I would rather muse on the Frost Fairs of old. From the twelfth century onwards there are reports of the river freezing solid. Between 1400 and the mid 1800s it was something that happened frequently.

There are reports of men on horseback being able to cross the river on the ice, of football matches, and of Elizabeth I taking regular strolls across her river. The first recorded Frost Fair was in 1607 when there were all manner of refreshment and entertainment booths on the frozen river, and by the middle of that century skating was popular. But the greatest Frost Fair of all was in the winter of 1683 to 1684, when the river froze to a depth of two feet for two months, and there were 'streets' of stalls. The last Frost Fair in the winter of 1813 to 1814 ended in disaster when the ice broke prematurely and people drowned in the icy waters as booths sank from view.

The river has never completely frozen since, due to the heat generated by the city, the discharging of effluent, and the upstream encroachment of tidal salt water. Only in the severe winter of 1963 did ice stretch right across the water, and that was up at Hampton Court.

Downstream is the Tower of London, with Traitor's Gate opening on to the water. Rowed into the Tower from the river, this gate would offer the likes of Anne Boleyn their last view of the outside world. The Tower dates from 1066, when building first began, but Tower Bridge, the Thames' most

The Albert Bridge across the Thames in London is a fine sight at night when thousands of light-bulbs illuminate its parapets and suspension cables.

Waterloo Bridge – one of a collection of river-crossings in the heart of London.

Maritime Museum. The grounds were originally laid out for Charles II by André le Notre, fresh from his triumph at Versailles.

A pedestrian tunnel under the river links Greenwich Pier with the Isle of Dogs. Once the Isle of Dogs was a green field, drained by dykes, then in 1802 the West India Docks were opened and this isthmus into the Thames took its place in London's bustling commerce. In the eighteenth and nineteenth centuries millions of tons of coal were unloaded here to make their way upriver. There was

famous bridge since the original London Bridge was dismantled and sold, is a Victorian edifice, opened by the Prince of Wales in 1894.

From the City of London, the river flows through the East End – through Bermondsey and Stepney, making a big loop to the south around the Isle of Dogs. The Port of London was once the greatest port in the world. Now it either sulks in decay or is being 'revitalised' by the construction of modern developments that make no use of the river, except as an aesthetic selling point on an estate agent's blurb.

The *Cutty Sark*, the famous clipper launched in 1869, is moored in dry dock outside the Royal Naval College at Greenwich, symbolic of the fact that the river is no longer an important navigational channel. The College was built by Wren in 1705 and the park is also the site of the Old Royal Observatory, where Greenwich Mean Time began in 1833, and the National

Will the Docklands ever pulsate as they once did? The Docklands express is a transport system that aims to put life back into the riverside.

trade in sugar and wool and even hay from Kent. Thousands of ships plied the river, loading and unloading a wide variety of goods, and employing thousands upon thousands of men. There were lightermen steering their barges, navvies using their brute force, and smugglers and thieves disappearing up Dickensian back-alleys with their booty. The docks themselves were constructed to exercise some control over the comings and goings of cargo.

The opening of Tilbury Docks downriver in the middle of the nineteenth century meant that larger ships could put in to unload. Thus began the decline of the London Docklands. Heavy bombing by the Luftwaffe during the Second World War almost a hundred years later sounded the death knell, and the last docks closed in 1981. The London Dockland Development Corporation was formed to mastermind the resurrection of a once thriving community, and London's tallest building, Canary Wharf on the Isle of Dogs, is visible for miles around, doing its best to tempt back commerce.

The 'S' bend around the Isle of Dogs takes the river to Woolwich and the site of the Thames Barrier. Stretching across the river, its silvered hoods looking like cast-offs from Sydney Opera House, it came into operation in 1982 after eight years of construction and a cost of £535 million.

For most folk, the Thames finishes at the flood barrier, but in reality it is still thirty miles from the sea. Even broader, it rolls on past Dagenham,

Erith and Grays, to Gravesend. It is at Gravesend that ships coming upstream take on their pilots, and opposite on the north bank of the river is Tilbury. Elizabeth I came here to rally her troops before they set out to fight the Spaniards, and the seventeenth-century fort was built as river protection. It is still the place from which cruise liners and freight ships come and go.

Now the river begins to widen more perceptibly towards the estuary. There are marshes on the south where wild-fowl and waders pick over the mud flats and saltings (marshland flooded at high tide). To the north is the industrial development of Canvey Island.

Essex man's resort of Southend-on-Sea is a sort of final marker for the Thames as it makes its way into the North Sea, joined, at Sheerness, by the River Medway. The two rivers flow either side of the Isle of Grain, where Pip encountered Magwitch in *Great Expectations,* and finally glide into the English Channel.

The Thames Flood Barrier; built at a cost of £535 million, it will hopefully prevent the repetition of floods that over the centuries have devastated the upper reaches of this historic river.

The Medway

Height at source: 450 feet
Length: 70 miles
Runs from Ashdown Forest to Sheerness

Pooh could get his chin on to the bottom rail if he wanted to, but it was more fun to lie down and get his head under it, and watch the river slipping slowly away beneath him.

from The House at Pooh Corner by A. A. Milne, 1885

There is a desolate quality to the Medway near this old fort on the Isle of Grain.

Iron deposits in the surrounding clays were excavated during the Iron Age and by the Romans, and in Tudor times the fast waters of the Medway and its many tributaries were used to power the wheels of forges – the energy being diverted into bellows and trip hammers that forged the iron. The Medway Valley was also quarried for Kentish ragstone, the stone used to build the Tower of London.

Thanks to its clayey origins, which produce an abundance of surface water, the Medway is very variable in flow. This variability is made use of by three reservoirs which store the excesses and even out the supply.

In the past the Medway had a reputation as a dirty river; surface water is easily polluted and, in 'the garden of England', fertiliser and other toxic agricultural waste could easily find its way into the water. Now, thanks to improved monitoring and restrictions on the discharging of waste and effluent, the prospect is brighter and the water much cleaner. Brown trout can be found upstream, as can grayling. The

The spring that will become the River Medway rises in the Ashdown Forest in Sussex, just above Turner's Hill, and makes its way across the Wealden clays past Winnie-the Pooh's bridge near Hartfield to be joined by the River Eden at Penshurst.

The origin of its name is most probably Celtic, being derived from *Medu*, meaning mead or sweet water.

upper reaches also support pike, roach and chub, and in the tributaries are bream, tench, dace and perch.

Flooding has been a problem in the past, especially in 1968 when Tonbridge suffered great damage. Now the largest flood storage area in Britain is positioned above Leigh to prevent any recurrence.

The Medway separates Kentish men (to the west of the river) from Men of Kent (to the east). Once there were plans to make the river navigable as far upstream as Penshurst, but the scheme foundered just beyond Tonbridge. The Norman castle at Tonbridge overlooks the river, and from here to Maidstone the Medway can be followed on the towpath through classic Kent countryside. William Cobbett, on one of his

It is easy to think of Rochester as just a noisy town that is swamped with traffic; but look hard and you will find remnants of its historic past - on the river and above.

Gillingham Strand where industry and waterfowl meet on the mudflats.

'Rural Rides', said of this stretch of country, 'I believe [it] to be the very finest, as to fertility and diminutive beauty, in the whole world.'

Outside Maidstone the river flows by Aylesford Priory, once a Carmelite Friary and still a popular place of pilgrimage. Then it snakes on to Rochester, Chatham and Gillingham, three towns that run into one another and which boast an impressive naval history. Elizabeth I founded the naval base at Chatham, and it still survives. Dickens lived here as a child and used the cathedral city of Rochester in his books more than any other place except London. The cathedral is Norman, though a cathedral has existed here since Saxon times. A Norman castle was built to defend the river in the reign of Henry I and it still stands.

The Medway widens into its own estuary at Gillingham where salt-marshes, meadows and mudflats support a variety of wildlife, from king-fishers and waders to sea lavender, bush crickets, marsh grasshoppers and dragonflies. Islands speckle the Medway estuary, which then joins the Thames estuary at Sheerness on the Isle of Sheppey, the ferry port for Vlissingen.

The waters of the two rivers mingle before breaking out into the North Sea. The Thames, which during the Ice Age was a tributary of the River Rhine, goes eastwards in search of its past to the sound of redshank, curlew and dunlin prospecting on the marshes and to the honk of Brent geese grazing the fields. It seems a long time since Moley rowed Ratty's boat on these same waters, underneath the willows.

The Test

Height at source: 275 feet
Length: 30 miles
Runs from Ashe to Southampton

They are not long rivers – the Test and Itchen – but long enough for men with unfevered blood in their veins to find sweet and peaceful homes on their margins.

from *Hampshire Days* by W. H. Hudson, 1923

Hudson, the countryman, was right about the peacefulness. Except where people have built weirs, the Test is a placid river. It never reaches the heights of spectacle achieved by more vigorous upland streams, but it has a matchless reputation when it comes to trout fishing.

The Test is a chalk stream whose waters have been filtered through subterranean layers of fine-grained limestone. The water takes a long time to seep through to the river so there are no rapid fluctuations in pace or depth at any time of year. The result is water that is as clear as gin.

Around my part of Hampshire the word 'Test' is spoken in hushed tones. For much of its length the fishing is private and pricey – over £1200 for a rod for the season – but then the Test is to trout fishing what Wimbledon is to lawn tennis. The funny thing is that when you watch the Test meandering through water meadows, quietly minding its own business, you wonder what all the fuss is about.

The river rises at Ashe, just a couple of miles north-west of Steventon where Jane Austen was born in 1775. Ashe, Deane and Steventon were Miss Austen's stamping ground for the first twenty-five years of her life. Her father was rector of Steventon but hunters for the rectory will be disappointed. All that marks the spot

The Test, the river that becomes England's finest trout-filled chalk stream, begins its life in pastures near the village of Ashe in Hampshire.

now is an iron pump in a field by the lane that leads up to the church; the house was demolished in the nineteenth century. The Lefroys, who lived in the rectory at Ashe, were good friends and Jane flirted with their son, Tom. Alas to no avail.

The tiny Church of St Nicholas at Steventon is the one Jane Austen knew but the Church of Holy Trinity and St Andrew at Ashe is not. It was rebuilt in 1877 and is the prettier of the two. Steventon Church is cement rendered but the church at Ashe is built with knapped flint. The soil is full of flints in these parts – Hampshire diamonds they call them. Ashe, itself, hardly merits the title of village. There is an imposing red-brick house, the church alongside a farm in a tree-filled hollow, and a cottage or two – and that is it.

The Test rises in pasture behind the church (but after heavy rain it can move higher up the valley). It then wends its way through Quidhampton and Overton before reaching Laverstoke and Whitchurch.

Now a village, Overton was a thriving town back in the sixteenth century with several fairs a year and a weekly market. In 1912 the last remaining annual fair sold 30,000 sheep. Like many old market towns, it is a deal quieter today. I always think of old villages as being higgledy-piggledy but look at a map of Overton and you see that is is built on a grid system. The Bishop of Winchester founded the 'new' town in 1217 and the mediaeval road layout dates from that time.

Round here the river is barely six inches deep and ten feet wide, except where it passes through large lagoons that were made for the paper mills. Reach into your pocket for a five pound note and you will be in touch with the River Test – every banknote has been washed in its waters. Henri Portal was a French refugee who reputedly fled from France hidden in a wine cask with his brother. He started his firm at Bere Mill in Whitchurch in 1712. When, in 1724, the Bank of England awarded him the contract to supply them with watermarked paper for their banknotes, he moved upriver

The White Hart Hotel at Whitchurch has a reminder that this is deer country.

Silk has been made at Whitchurch Silk Mill since 1830 and is still manufactured today. The mill stands on Frog Island in the middle of the Test.

Whitchurch is the first real town on the Test: a busy little bottleneck where six roads meet. Whitchurch Silk Mill stands on Frog Island in the middle of the river. The building dates from 1800, and its clock from 1815 when it was erected to Celebrate Wellington's victory at the Battle of Waterloo. The river still turns the mill wheel, and silk has been made here since 1830. You can see how it is done; the mill is open to visitors.

The countryside around here is gently rolling with plenty of beech woods and pasture, and at Hurstbourne Priors, where the Bourne rivulet flows into the Test, fishing begins in earnest.

Longparish is the village where the Test Way footpath picks up the river. Perversely it starts at Inkpen in Wiltshire and makes its way down the Bourne Valley before following the Test from Longparish to Totton near Southampton. It is forty-six miles long and for much of its length takes the route of the old railway line.

From here on the river frequently divides and then meets up with itself again, so that there are always at least two and sometimes as many as four rivulets, all snaking their way through the watermeadows. Longparish is well named; the village is a couple of miles long, following the run of the river, with cottages that may be white painted and cement rendered, or of knapped flint. Many have thatched roofs.

Ask about local characters in these parts and they will tell you about Colonel Peter Hawker who fought with

Thatched cottages predominate in Wherwell (pronounced 'Werrell' by the locals). An abbey, built here in the tenth century, lasted until the dissolution.

to Laverstoke. Portals, now at their Overton Mill, still make the paper, using water taken from a spring. It is returned to the Test cleaner than when it was extracted, says the company. Considering the fine fishing further downstream, I suppose there is no arguing with this. But I like the sound of William Cobbett who used to pass by on his *Rural Rides* railing in the direction of the mill: 'I hope the time will come when a monument will be erected where that mill stands... inscribed *the curse of England*.' Cobbett was not a fan of paper money.

One thing that catches your eye in Laverstoke is a row of thatched and half-timbered cottages at the side of the main road. Historic they may look, but were built in 1939.

There are watercress beds around here and their crunchy green produce is shipped all over the country. There are watermeadows, too – tracts of land that were once flooded with warm river water in the early months of the year to promote rapid grass growth. It is a system that is no longer a part of modern farm practice, even in villages where time has stood still.

The gardens at Longstock Park were developed between 1946 and 1953 and rank as some of the loveliest water gardens in the country. Sheets of clear water, fed by the River Test, boast carp and dragonflies and a tremendous variety of aquatic and bog plants.

the Duke of Wellington. After a bullet put paid to his military ambitions in the Peninsular War, he took out his revenge on the wildlife of the area. He lived in Longparish House and his Diary (written between 1809 and 1853 and first published in 1893) details the exploits of a man who enjoyed putting paid to anything that moved. In the first week of September 1815 he shot ninety partridges, eleven hares, two quail, a snipe and a rabbit. His forays on the river were equally merciless and he even committed the cardinal sin of fishing for trout with minnows – guaranteed to make a fly fisherman turn a dangerous shade of puce.

Past Harewood Forest, the Test flows through Bransbury Common. In 1924 this area was described by Harry Plunket Greene in *Where the Bright Waters Meet* as 'one of the most romantic spots in the South of England'. The river then carries on between two picturesque villages, Chilbolton and Wherwell (pronounced Werrell). Miss Marple would approve of these villages – they are very much in the St Mary Meade mould.

Wherwell was once the site of an abbey, founded in 986 by Queen Elfreda, widow of King Edgar. It was a nunnery where the wives of noblemen were often sent on retreat (whether they felt like retreating or not). Both King Cnut and Edward the Confessor sent their wives here. The abbey lasted until the dissolution. Now nothing of it remains beside the Victorian church where it once stood. The present Wherwell Priory is a nineteenth-century house.

Chilbolton mixes old and new. The thatched cottages are old and the Chilbolton Observatory, with its satellite dish, is relatively new, though it occupies an airfield where Spitfires were assembled and tested during the Second World War. Chilbolton Common is an area much prized by botanists for its rich variety of grasses but listen out for the drumming of snipe among the hay.

At West Down the River Anton joins the Test and it is here that two other modes of transportation once were found. The Andover Canal was opened in 1794 to take produce from Andover to Southampton. It operated until 1857, though never with great success, and was superseded by a railway known locally as the 'Sprat and Winkle Line'.

The railway opened in 1865, joining the Salisbury to Southampton line at Kimbridge. Twenty years later another line was opened running from Hurstbourne through Longparish and Wherwell to Fullerton. This Northern and Southern Junction Railway was nicknamed 'The Nile'. It lasted until 1956 and had a chequered career that included it being used as a prop in the 1927 film of Arnold Ridley's *Ghost Train*, and as a means for carrying munitions to a dump in Harewood Forest during the last war. The Sprat and Winkle Line fell, like so many others, under Dr Beeching's axe in the early 1960s. Travelling through this scenery, a journey along this line must have been one to treasure.

The village of Leckford comes next down the river. It is worth a nod in its direction simply because it was bought, lock, stock and fishing rights, by John Lewis in 1928 and is now used as a holiday village for employees (sorry, partners) of the John Lewis Partnership. The Partnership also owns Longstock Park Gardens, across the river from Leckford. This is one of the finest water gardens in the country and dates from the 1940s. There are specimen shrubs and trees here, too. The gardens are open only half a dozen times during the year but catch them if you can.

At this point the Test is fifteen miles from Southampton Water but this did not prevent the Danes from locating a construction and maintenance yard for their long ships here. The prospect of long ships wending their way through the Hampshire countryside is an odd one but centuries ago it did happen.

There are different sights around Longstock today for photographers to sigh over. Bridges and sluices cross the river, and there are circular thatched huts on islands. These romantic-looking fishing shelters are linked to the banks with plank bridges that support eel traps which can be lowered into the water. Eels like young trout so fishermen do not like eels.

Stockbridge ranks as the heart of trout fishing country. The wide main street – the Winchester to Salisbury road – is criss-crossed by streams,

Thatched fishermen's huts provide access to eel traps on the most picturesque part of the River Test near Longstock where the river-bank vegetation is at its most lush.

Ducks enjoy the rivulets of the River Test that flow under Stockbridge High Street.

The Grosvenor Hotel at Stockbridge has a broad, covered entrance porch, built to allow coaches to discharge their passengers without them getting wet. It is here that the Houghton Club meets – reputedly the most exclusive angling club in the world. Upstairs in the clubroom there are old leather chairs, portraits of fishermen and their catches, and stuffed fish in glass cases affixed to the walls.

Much of the reputation of this stretch of the river is due to William Lunn. He started life in the second half of the nineteenth century as a keeper's boy on a Surrey estate, later becoming a messenger in a London bank. He was spotted by the secretary of the Houghton Club who encouraged him to become a river keeper. Lunn moved into Riverside Cottage beside Sheepbridge Shallows at Houghton in 1887, and lived there until he died. His son, Alf, and his grandson, Mick, took on the job of river keeper after him.

William Lunn was the supreme naturalist and worked out how to conserve the mayfly, whose population (vital to the survival of trout) was dwindling. By introducing more reliable methods of larval hatching he improved the trout population and brought this stretch of the river its matchless reputation.

The craft of river keeper is one that combines acute observation with biological knowledge and a keen sense of timing. The keeper must cut weed to prevent the channel silting up. He must manage the stew ponds where young trout are raised, also the hatching,

furnished at all times of year with mallard. There are shops selling home-made pies and pasties, jams and chutney, fishing tackle and antiques. The petrol pumps at the side of the road are of the old kind, with great swinging arms that cross the top of your vehicle if you have parked with your filler cap on the wrong side. Folk serve you here with a smile and a merry quip in a Hampshire burr.

A hundred years ago, this part of the country was famous for racehorses as well as fishing. There was a race-course between Danebury Down, where the Danebury Ring Iron Age Hill Fort stands, and Chattis Hill. They used to race on Houghton Down and Stockbridge Down. From John Day's Danebury stables in the nineteenth century came three Derby winners, four winners of The Oaks and the Two Thousand Guineas, and one St Leger winner. Nine racing stables were here at one time, but with improved road transport, and access to grander courses at Newbury and Ascot, the racing died out. But there are reminders of this glorious past. One is Hermit Lodge which was named after a horse that won the Derby in 1877 – in a snowstorm at odds of 100–1.

matching and despatching of the fish. He must see to the conservation of the river banks and the pollarding of trees, all with the aim of ensuring that, come April, when the angler casts his first fly, there will be something to offer him good sport.

South of Stockbridge, near the river, is Marsh Court – a house with tall chimneys, designed by Sir Edwin Lutyens. It is white not because it is painted but because it is built of chalk. The garden, designed by Gertrude Jekyll, is being restored to its former glory by the Hampshire Gardens Trust.

The river flows through the village of Houghton that gives its name to the angling club, and past Kings Somborne and Horsebridge. Peat has been dug here in the past which accounts for the presence of a large lake near Marsh Court. This is an area rich in bird life. Reed and sedge warblers breed alongside the water, and nightingales have been recorded in the woodland. Gadwall overwinter here.

It is the perfect setting for Mottisfont Abbey, a thirteenth-century priory which prospered until the time of the Black Death, after which it never

Rampant bears adorn the gates of Mottisfont Abbey.

Edwin Lutyens and Gertrude Jekyll worked together designing many houses and gardens in England, including Marsh Court near Stockbridge. Built of chalk, with red brick chimneys, it dates from 1901 and the Jekyll garden that surrounds it is being restored.

A five-span seventeenth-century bridge crosses the River Test at Redbridge as well as a more modern road bridge. There has been a crossing point here for centuries and the estuary is flanked by marshes – hence the earlier name of 'Reed bridge'. The bridges here were frequently covered by tides and the crossing became a hazardous undertaking.

Did King John come here? An old hunting lodge in Romsey bears his name and the date 1250.

fully recovered. Much of what you see today dates from the eighteenth century, though the house was acquired at the dissolution by the Lord Chamberlain and parts of it date back to those Tudor times. It is a handsome, mellow brick building with stone quoins. During the summer you can watch Shakespearean plays in the garden and, if you time your visit during late June or early July, you can admire the spectacular flowering of the national collection of old-fashioned shrub roses, amassed by the enthusiast Graham Stuart Thomas. The Augustinian canons have now been replaced as custodians by the National Trust.

Four miles south of Mottisfont is Romsey, the grandest town on the Test. Dominated by its abbey, there is very much the feel of a market town about Romsey. The abbey was originally established by Benedictine nuns in the tenth century but was ransacked by the Danes at the beginning of the eleventh century. The present abbey dates from the twelfth century. It is a solid, angular, pale grey building, regarded as having one of the finest Norman churches in Britain. Lord Mountbatten is buried here.

Even in the nineteenth century changes were afoot in Romsey Abbey. In 1845 the Reverend Edward Berthon removed bricks and rubble from internal archways (placed there earlier to reduce draughts). He also devised a scheme whereby two stained-glass windows could be lowered so their tops once more came into view.

A technical wizard, Berthon invented a collapsible boat made from wood and canvas. Manufactured by the 'Berthon Boat Company', these portable boats were widely used as liferafts, and could be found on ocean-going liners until 1912. They fell badly out of favour at this time, having been used unsuccessfully on a ship called *The Titanic*.

There is much to see in Romsey. King John's House is a timbered, tile-roofed dwelling thought to be a thirteenth-century hunting lodge. The Swan Inn, now the Conservative Club, still has an old wrought-iron sign from which General Fairfax hanged two of his soldiers found guilty of drunkenness and murder in 1642. And in the market place is a statue of the Victorian prime minister, Lord Palmerston.

Palmerston it was who owned Broadlands, the stately pile situated to the south of the town and latterly known as the home of Lord Mountbatten of Burma, the last Viceroy of India. It was here that the Prince and Princess of Wales began their honeymoon. Now the home of Lord Romsey, the house shows evidence both of Palmerston and Mountbatten; house and grounds have been open to the public since 1979. The stable block is devoted to an exhibition reflecting the lives of Lord and Lady Mountbatten – a pageant of pomp and riches, influence and connection, encompassing everything from garter robes to stately limousines.

There has been a house on this site for four hundred years but the current Palladian mansion was built in the eighteenth century. Among the 'Capability' Brown landscape you can find trees that were planted at the insistence of Lord Mountbatten by famous visitors who came to Broadlands – everyone from Charlie Chaplin to Grace Kelly. The River Test runs through the grounds and it is here that the Prince of Wales learned to fish under the tuition of the river keeper, Bernard Aldrich. In his book, *The Ever Rolling Stream*, Aldrich admits that Lord Mountbatten was not a keen fisherman. He recalls one occasion when, with a ten-year-old Prince Charles and a younger Princess Anne in tow, he

Southampton's seafaring history dates back to the Romans. Although badly bombed during the Second World War, some ancient architecture survives – like the old city walls and the Wool House, seen here. Built in the fourteenth century, it was used in the eighteenth century to house Spanish prisoners-of-war. Now it is a maritime museum.

assisted his employer in catching a salmon under one of the estate bridges. Alas, Lord Louis let the fish slip off the hook, only to be told by Prince Charles, 'My Daddy wouldn't have lost the fish.'

Salmon have been caught in the Test as far up as Longparish but it is south of Romsey, between Nursling and Lee where the river makes one concentrated stream, that they are to be found in greatest numbers. Over the years these numbers have declined greatly. At one time a couple of thousand salmon could be caught each year between the M27 at Nursling and Romsey; now fishermen are lucky if they catch a hundred. Once a salmon weighing 43 pounds and 3 feet 10 inches long, with a girth of 2 feet $11\frac{1}{2}$ inches, was caught here but netting of the breeding grounds near Greenland have put paid to such trophies. Even so, the National Rivers Authority and the river keepers on the various 'beats' of the Test do their bit to make sure that conditions remain as favourable as possible both for salmon and trout.

Time was when the river keepers on the Upper Test regarded salmon as vermin and a danger to their beloved trout. There were even moves to have a blockade across the river at Sadler's Mill to prevent the salmon from running above Romsey.

Nursling is the site of the earliest Christian activity in Hampshire and St Boniface travelled to Germany from the monastery here. No trace of the monastery remains in this hamlet which was originally called Nutshalling, meaning 'the nut grove by the water meadows'.

South of Nursling, on the way to Redbridge, is a large expanse of reed beds. Thatch is cut here, and reed and sedge warblers breed. This is an area rich in bird and plant life, from bearded tits and booming bitterns to wild celery and orchids. Wildfowl over-winter here in large numbers: redshank, dunlin, mallard, teal, widgeon and curlew. Not surprisingly, 270 acres of this countryside form a nature reserve managed by the Hampshire and Isle of Wight Naturalists' Trust.

Redbridge (originally Reedbridge) has been a crossing point of the River Test for centuries. It was once the point at which timber from the New Forest was loaded onto ships bound for the naval dockyards. Below this suburb of Southampton and the neighbouring town of Totton, the Test ceases to be a romantic chalk stream, flanked by cottages of flint and thatch. It broadens, has mudflats at its banks, and turns, gradually, into Southampton Water. From here it flows into Britain's most southerly channel, The Solent.

Its leafy banks and trout filled waters but a memory, the River Test flows out into the sea through the docklands of Southampton.

The Exe

Height at source: 1500 feet
Length: 55 miles
Runs from Exe Head to Exmouth

Child, if they ask who killed thee,
Say it was the Doones of Badgworthy.

Anon

It was in the seventeenth century that the notorious Doone family made Exmoor unsafe to roam, and R. D. Blackmore romanticised the legend with *Lorna Doone* in 1869. From 1620 to 1699 the Doones terrorised families in these parts, sparing neither women nor children as the above rhyme recalls. Eventually the locals rebelled and routed the nefarious villains, who fled Exmoor for good.

On a winter's day on Exe Head you can look towards Badgworthy, two or three hills away, with screwed-up eyes as the horizontal rain stings your cheeks. It is weather guaranteed to make the most placid of people tetchy.

That great nineteenth-century naturalist, Richard Jefferies, remarked: 'The moors of the Exe river are not flat stretches of marshland, but hills of great height covered with heather.' Today many tracts of Exmoor have no heather at all, probably as a result of overgrazing.

There are no wanted posters to warn you of the Doones today. There is only a sign that reads:

Exford is a country village famous for its stag hounds, Exmoor pony shows and for fishing in the waters of the Exe. The ford has long since gone, but the village is still a popular watering place for travellers.

Pack-horse bridges, like this one at Winsford, are frequent on the Exe. Their pink-tinged stones look rosier still in a Devon sunset.

Under close control and regularly wormed your dog is welcome on Exmoor. Uncontrolled, loose and unwormed it isn't.

The sign stands right by the infant Exe near Blackpitts Gate, half a mile from Exe Head where the river has its boggy, peaty source.

Here sheep with their backs to the driving rain close crop the fine moor-land grass between the tussocks in this treeless landscape, while the young river snakes its way along the valley bottom between woolly fields that slope steeply on either side. It is as clear as a moorland stream should be. Running over pebbles of amber and ochre it is cold and crisp to the touch.

Doone Country, as marked on the map, is three miles to the north-east where Badgworthy Water runs into

East Lyn River. The Exe, though, runs eastwards, before deciding on a southerly course down to Exeter and the sea at Exmouth.

The roads around this part of Somerset (Devon does not begin until Exbridge, about twelve miles away) are sheltered by steep banks on either side, frequently topped by beech hedges that keep their coppery leaves in winter and shed them as the new buds burst in spring. No one knows for sure when these boundaries between adjacent lands were constructed, but even today the winding lanes zig-zag between them rather than carve them up. The banks sport all manner of wild flowers, from ferns and mosses to the round-leaved pennywort.

The disadvantage of these towering banks is that they make it mighty

difficult for the walker or motorist to admire the West Country views, except through gateways or rare gaps in the hedges. But at least they reduce the power of the wind.

The Exe takes its name from the Celtic *Eisca*, meaning a river full of fish. And it is. The trout are prized, and where the red deer and ponies of Exmoor pause to drink there are young salmon in the crystal clear waters of the stream. Where the water speeds up you can see dippers – birds like giant wrens with chestnut bellies and white bibs, dipping into the water for food or even showing their superiority over run-of-the-mill waterfowl by walking underwater on the riverbed. They swallow stones for ballast. Buzzards wheel in the sky and there are black grouse here, too.

The village of Exton clings to the side of a hill and offers fine views across the valley. Everything is on a slope here.

From the moor the river flows down through the combes of Wellshead and Riscombe, under hump-backed bridges of grey-pink stone. Now there are trees along its banks and sheep graze the riverside meadows. Woodland begins to climb the sides of the valley. We are still in Somerset but this is what you might call typical Devon scenery – soft and rolling, the river at its heart and dry stone walls and hedges enclosing every fold.

More water joins the river from tributaries such as Allcombe Water and Greenland Water before it flows through the village of Exford.

The ford is no more and a stone bridge carries the traffic. The village is renowned as a centre for stag hunting and fishing; there are horse shows here, too, on the last Sunday in May and later in summer when you can see the best of Exmoor ponies. There is a triangular green in the centre of Exford, but it is not what you might call a chocolate box village – which, as far as the residents are concerned, ranks as a plus.

The sheep around here must have two long legs and two short ones, to be able to graze the steep slopes on either side of Larcombe Brook. This joins the Exe at the next village downriver, Winsford.

Ernest Bevin, the wartime Minister of Labour, was born in Winsford. Like Exford, it nestles in a hollow and has its church on a hill. Unlike Exford, it still has a ford. There are six, seven or eight bridges in this village depending on whom you talk to. There is also a fifteenth-century malt house – Karstal

Few country town churches are as large or as beautiful and ornate as St Peter's, Tiverton, whose stone is a warm shade of pink.

House – converted into a hotel, and a mile out of the village at Spire Cross is the Caractacus Stone. This is a monolith of unknown origin, thought by some to have been erected as a memorial to King Caractacus who stood up to the Romans in AD 50. It was used as a forest boundary as long ago as 1219.

It is worth a three-mile detour from the Exe at Winsford to look at Tarr Steps over the nearby River Barle. Like the Caractacus Stone, the origins of this 180-foot stone-slab clapper bridge are lost in the mists of time. The stones are not from round these parts and some say that the bridge dates from prehistoric times (though it had to be rebuilt after the floods of 1952).

More recent forces have been at work on a sign by the roadside in Winsford. Someone has pinched the letter 'h' and, at the time of writing, the sign reads 'Beware peasants on road'.

Exton clings to the side of a hill above the river, its pastures retained by towering banks that cascade with water in wet winter weather. Down below, the banks of the river are well wooded – through Bridgetown, past Chilly Bridge to Exebridge. Just above Exebridge, the River Haddeo joins the Exe, bringing water reserves from Wimbleball Reservoir, and then the Barle flows into it.

The Barle is the better river for salmon fishing but the Exe, too,

Inside St Peter's Church in Tiverton, in the year 1844, Mendelssohn's Wedding March received its first performance at a marriage service.

Honiton and Exeter. The Exe is relatively free of pollution but its spates can turn the water extremely muddy. It is a reliable sort of river. The Water Authority can maintain minimum levels in the Exe and still have enough to top up the River Taw in summer when necessary. There are weirs at Bolham and another tributary joins the fray, but greater beauty is to be found off the main road at a place called Knightshayes Court.

Here fifty acres of garden surround the warm red sandstone house which matches the soil in these parts. 'The Garden in the Wood' was created by Sir John and Lady Heathcoat Amory after the last war and has plants that will make enthusiasts drool. A topiary fox is being chased by hounds, rich woodland provides shelter that makes the growing easy for tender plants, and there is a famous pool garden. It is worth a detour.

Tiverton is an ancient up-and-down town, probably a Saxon settlement in the seventh century, and has a twelfth-century castle in blushing pinkish-grey stone. The castle stands on the banks of the Exe and was occupied by the Earls of Devon until the sixteenth century. The river is broad here and moves swiftly through this town which shows architectural evidence of its days as a place of wool manufacture. Coarse ribbed cloth called kersey was woven here until the woollen trade died out in the nineteenth century. Then lace-making took over, thanks to the arrival of John Heathcoat who brought his bobbinett machine with him when the

supports them. Juveniles are found as far up as the source but the main salmon stretch of the Exe is between Exebridge and Countess Wear at Exeter, with trout and some grayling between Exebridge and Tiverton.

South of Bampton the River Batherm adds its waters to the spate and the now robust Exe heads south for Tiverton.

Just as you are wondering where all this water could possibly be going, at Bolham, on the outskirts of Tiverton, is a pumping station making use of the hearty river to supply Tiverton,

Otters are now seen in the Exe and Taw but their real stronghold in Devon is still further west in the catchment area of the River Torridge.

Luddite riots forced him to leave Leicester. Tiverton lace is still used for the bridal veils of royal princesses.

Tiverton's place on the educational map is assured; Peter Blundell founded Blundell's School here in 1599, and R. D. Blackmore was educated at the Old School. It still stands near the bridge over the River Lowman which joins the Exe south of the town.

The Parish Church of St Peter is a delight. Like the Castle it has blushing stone, and on its fine organ, Mendelssohn's Wedding March was first played for a wedding in 1844.

Above the town to the east is another waterway, an arm of the Grand Western Canal. This was the canal intended to link the Bristol and English Channels but, in spite of this eleven-mile stretch built between 1810 and 1814, the job was never completed. It seems strange to see a canal supported by huge, pink buttressed stone walls, scaled by several flights of steps. The view from its banks, high over the town, is panoramic. The brightly coloured narrowboats of the Grand Western Horse Boat Company float on water that is flanked by broad grass verges, and horses pull them between Tiverton and Loudwalls through the Grand Western Canal Country Park.

Past Tiverton the Exe flows to Bickleigh, whose whitewashed, thatched cottages on the river bank draw photographers like bees to blossom. The mill on the Exe at Bickleigh, with its river-powered millwheel, has become a craft and fishing centre, and around it a farm specialising in ancient breeds still uses shirehorses for ploughing and the like.

The Exe is crossed by a sixteenth-century bridge (rebuilt in 1809 after

At Bickleigh the river has undeniably picturesque qualities. Even the Ordnance Survey map carries its picture on the cover.

The Exe

flooding). On the opposite bank to the mill is the Trout Inn, a thatched seventeenth-century hostelry, and the ruins of Bickleigh Castle, a Norman fortification that Fairfax, on behalf of Cromwell, knocked about a bit. The surviving eleventh-century chapel is reckoned by many to be the oldest building in Devon.

The Manor House, built on the site of the castle, was the home of the Carews – a distinguished family which included Vice-Admiral Sir George Carew. He commanded the *Mary Rose*, Henry VIII's flagship which sank off Portsmouth in full view of the King in 1545. 'I have the sort of knaves I cannot rule,' are said to have been his last words. Nobody argued the point then or since.

The landscape broadens out after the steep slopes of Bickleigh to become gently rolling with pasture on all sides, and the enclosed feeling of the Exe Valley disappears. The wide, full river is now bound for Exeter, the county town of Devon. Before it enters the city it is joined by the River Culm which once contained even more industrial waste than it does now. Things are improving slowly.

Badly damaged though it was in the Second World War, Exeter is still rich in architecture, with a superb cathedral, commercial buildings and houses in an assortment of styles. The river runs through it like a main artery. Until 1282 the town was a busy port, but then Isabella de Fortibus, a Countess of Devon, was offended by the people of Exeter and had a weir built across the

The Custom House – one of the first buildings in Exeter to be made of brick in 1685.

river so that navigation became impossible. Instead, vessels had to put in at Topsham, further downriver, which fattened Isabella's purse considerably. By the time the weir was removed, around three hundred years later, the river was too silted up to take heavy traffic. The Exeter Ship Canal was excavated to replace it and now runs alongside, fed by sluices. Up here came cargoes of ore, timber, coal, sugar, spices and tobacco from Europe and the Americas. Woollen cloth was exported.

When first dug by John Trew in 1560 the canal was only 3 feet deep and 14 feet wide. Boats had to be hauled through it not by horses, for there was no towing path, but by men known as 'halers'. In 1676 the canal was extended as far as Topsham and by 1701 it had been deepened to 10 feet and widened to 50 feet. The labouring was done by a team of workers which included '200 women all in white, with clean straw hats, armed with mattocks and shovels, with drums beating and the city music playing before them.'

The handsome Custom House on Exeter Quay, completed in 1685, was the first major brick building in the city.

The River Exe still seems to burst into life at Exeter. The canal and quays may no longer handle the type of commerce they did between the sixteenth and eighteenth centuries but the warehouses are now the site of a thriving Maritime Museum, and on the water outside are vessels like the Danish tugboat *St Canute*, built in 1931. The river bustles today not with cargoes but with leisure activities, from canoeing and pleasure boating to sailing and fishing. The Quay House that once sheltered goods as they were loaded and unloaded now serves as a convenient information centre.

At Trew's Weir, constructed in 1564 to increase the depth of the canal, leats were made to power a mill which was still producing paper as late as 1982. Other factories situated alongside the

Topsham has a real fishing village atmosphere and near the Passage House Inn a ferry still crosses the River Exe. It is a place of ship's chandlers, merchants' houses and taverns that reek of Long John Silver – well almost.

river were used mainly for flax milling, clothmaking, bell founding, tanning and sugar refining.

In the 1820s and 1830s the canal was extended to Turf, near Powderham, by James Green, in spite of huge problems with collapsing mudbanks and destructive tides. By the end of the nineteenth century, however, the arrival of the railways and the reduction in water traffic brought about its decline. Today, cormorants sit on the sluice gates and locks, and moorhens dabble in the water. The Riverside Valley Park is a seven-mile stretch of the Exe which teems with wildlife, from kingfishers, herons and snipe to butterflies and newts, occupying the varied wildlife habitats that exist here.

There is game and coarse fishing on the river and coarse fishing on the canal. Above Countess Wear are salmon, and coarse fishing in the river here yields bream, roach, dace, chub, perch and pike. The Exe has no appreciable run of sea trout though there are some grayling, which is unusual in the south-west. Keen birders can rise at 4.30 am in May to hear the dawn chorus, and children with nets can go pond dipping in summer. These sorties, and others, are arranged by the town's department of leisure and tourism.

If you want to know the time while you are in Exeter, head towards the river and the church of St Mary-at-Steppes. Its three-hundred-year-old clock, with a face showing the four seasons, has mechanical painted figures to strike the hours.

There is a peaceful feeling in Exmouth. It is a quaint town where the Esplanade has a flavour and tranquility of Victorian days.

As you follow the Exe towards the sea from Exeter, the first port of call is Topsham which, in spite of its close proximity to the city, retains its village charm. The River Clyst flows into the Exe here and there are plenty of traces of Topsham's days as an important port. Today the vessels are yachts and cruisers – the village's fishing fleet is a thing of the past – but plenty of boatyards are needed to supply and service these craft.

Topsham is everyone's idea of a fishing village, even if the salmon are now caught in much smaller numbers. Figureheads sprout from the corners of buildings, and dog-legged alleyways run between half-timbered, black-and-white cottages and a plenitude of characterful pubs.

Ships' nails were once made here and Sir William Follett, the youngest Englishman ever to become Attorney General, was born in Follett Lodge. There are ship's chandlers, Topsham Sailing Club (founded in 1888), and the handsome Georgian Globe Hotel. Near the Passage House Inn a passenger ferry crosses the river, and there are views across the beginnings of the estuary from the row of merchants' houses known as the Strand.

Downriver from Topsham, the Exe is tidal and the estuary gradually widens. On the western side is Powderham Castle, home of the Courtenays, Earls of Devon. It has one of Devon's largest heronries and parkland where fallow deer browse. Originally mediaeval, the existing building dates in parts from the fourteenth to the nineteenth centuries. Powderham Church is fifteenth century and stands in its red sandstone glory on the edge of the estuary.

The railway line from Exeter St Davids to Dawlish Warren runs alongside the estuary from Powderham onwards, and the trip by train is worth taking. This was Isambard Kingdom Brunel's 'Atmospheric Railway'. Nothing to do with the stunning scenery, the title refers to Brunel's system of assisting traction by vacuum suction on a central pipe, from which the air was sucked by pumping houses at intervals along the line. It was unsuccessful (rodents gnawing at the leather seals didn't help) and the route was eventually operated with conventional locomotives. At Starcross the only surviving pumping station has been turned into a museum. The railway on the opposite side of the river (from Exeter to Exmouth via Topsham) has good views, too. South of Topsham it runs through Lympstone, a pretty fishing village whose church has a handsome mediaeval red sandstone tower. On the mudflats and in the reed beds between

Dawlish Warren once supported only rabbits; now it is a nature reserve.

Breakwaters at Dawlish Warren. The Exe flows into the English Channel here, past sandy beaches that are as much a home to birds as holidaymakers.

the two sides of the estuary even the most casual twitcher can spot an incredibly rich variety of birdlife.

At Exebridge, across the water from Topsham, other reed beds are home to warblers, starlings and swallows, often preyed upon by hobby and sparrowhawk. Dragonflies abound in summer and waders enjoy the shelter in winter. There are waders at Powderham, too – greenshank and dunlin among them – and the estuary is also enjoyed in winter by that rarest of birds, the avocet.

There are two sentinels at the point where the Exe meets the sea: Exmouth, on the eastern side, and Dawlish Warren on the west.

Exmouth is a quaint town. The oldest seaside resort in Devon, it has Georgian, Victorian and Edwardian architecture, and a sedate Esplanade of white- and cream-painted houses. The centre of the town bustles like any

When the sun is slipping slowly into the west and the cloud formation is favourable, it is easy to see why artists such as J.M.W. Turner took the trouble to set up their easels at the mouth of the Exe to capture the sunsets. It is a peaceful exit for a river that has tumbled down the rugged slopes of Exmoor.

other but everywhere there are reminders of a slower age. The Beacon is a terrace of Georgian houses in which lived both Lady Byron (No. 19) and Lady Nelson (No. 6) during the early part of the nineteenth century.

The sandy beaches and red cliffs still attract tourists, and from the Esplanade they can look across to Dawlish Warren, until two hundred years ago a safe haven for rabbits.

Although tourism has invaded, with its caravans and ice-cream kiosks, the Dawlish Warren Nature Reserve occupies 505 acres of floral and ornithological riches. Yellow bartsia, eyebright and evening primrose grow among the scrub on this 'sandy spit' which pushes its way almost across the mouth of the estuary. There are dragonflies and crickets here in summer, along with gulls, terns, oystercatchers and cormorants. In winter Brent geese, mergansers and many different wading birds are seen. Bobbing on the water are teal, pintail and widgeon.

It is heartening when a river can go out in a blaze of glory and the Exe certainly does that. It flows into the English Channel among a richness of wildlife that is hard to beat, and sunsets of a brilliance that inspired J. M. W. Turner to set up his easel.

The Tamar

Height at source: 700 feet
Length: 60 miles
Runs from Woolley to Plymouth

The Tamar, which for nearly all its course divides Devon and Cornwall, is a river that, in the matter of size, ranks with the Dart and Exe. But as regards its estuary, being the principal affluent of Plymouth harbour, acquires by this a distinction far above these other streams of purely local fame.

from *The Rivers and Streams of England* by A. G. Bradley, 1909

It is thanks to the River Tamar that Cornwall and the Cornish retained their independence from the rest of England until only a thousand years ago. It was in 815 that the Celtic Britons of Cornwall were attacked and eventually defeated by King Egbert of Wessex. Later they rose up with Viking support but were finally crushed at Hingston Down near Gunnislake. But for the Tamar they would have been overpowered sooner.

There is still a feeling of individuality about the folk of Cornwall. Daphne du Maurier noticed it:

There is in the Cornish character, smouldering beneath the surface, ever ready to ignite, a fiery independence, a stubborn pride.

Until the early nineteenth century the Cornish language survived. It is all down to the river.

The Tamar rises just eastwards of Woolley, a hamlet in the parish of Morwenstow, presided over between 1835 and 1874 by the cleric and poet,

The Tamar is channelled into lakes early in its life. Wildfowl make the most of them.

the Revd Robert Stephen Hawker. Over the door of Morwenstow Vicarage, built by Hawker, is inscribed the following motto:

*A House, a Glebe, a Pound a Day,
A Pleasant Place to Watch and Pray;
Be true to Church, Be kind to Poor,
O Minister, for evermore.*

The source is barely four miles from the village of Morwenstow and the north Cornish coast – a rugged coast which, in Hawker's day, would regularly claim ships and men. Hawker buried the bodies that were unidentified under a ship's figurehead which still stands in the churchyard.

The first bridge over the southern-flowing Tamar is no more than a concrete pipe, located in a wooded valley before the stream flows down between West and East Youlstone to the two Tamar Lakes. These are vast sheets of water with uses both practical and pleasurable.

The now rare barn owl frequents the countryside around the upper Tamar river.

The Upper Tamar Lake is the youngest. A reservoir whose dam was completed as recently as 1975, it is the larger of the two lakes. You can fish for rainbow trout here or paddle your own canoe. There is coarse fishing on the Lower Tamar Lake which is a rich nature reserve, originally created to feed the Bude Canal in 1820. Here are swans, geese and ducks, including divers like goosander and goldeneye. Waders such as sandpiper and snipe probe the muddy shores with their bills. Kingfishers sport on the feeder streams, and dragonflies and damsel flies whirr above the water. In winter there are merlins, hen harriers and gulls. Barn owls and buzzards are seen here, too, as well as the otter.

This rare mammal is a classic sign of a healthy river – a river in which the water is pure enough to suit it and the fish on which it feeds. The right river-bank habitat must also be present. The River Torridge, about five miles to the east of the Tamar, is the otter's stronghold in this area and boasts a healthy population in eighty per cent of its catchment area.

The Tamar is a lowland stream, flowing through farmland, and the banning of residual and toxic chemicals should do much to improve the fifteen miles of the Upper Tamar which have been adversely affected by farm pollution and abstraction. These have so damaged the salmon spawning that to maintain the Tamar as one of the country's premier salmon rivers, 30,000 juveniles are annually released into the waters. It still has good runs of

The church of St Bridget at Bridgerule dates from the fifteenth century. The walls inside are elaborately decorated and the floor is of chequered Cornish slate.

salmon and sea trout in spring and summer, as the fish make their way up from the sea. The trout are also known for their size – larger than average thanks to the fact that the stream is only mildly acid, flowing through farmland rather than moorland. One day I hope the balance will be right for all parties.

The Bude Canal, whose feeder comes out of the Lower Tamar Lake alongside the river, was begun in 1819. It was used to transport calcium-rich sand from Bude to the farming communities inland as far as Launceston, where it was used as fertiliser. The canal was the longest ever to be built for the use of tub boats. These amazing vessels had wheels so that when they reached one of the six inclined planes on the canal's route they could be pulled on rails up the smooth hillsides. They were then refloated on the canal at the top. This system was an alternative to high-rise locks but it had its problems. Occasionally the chains holding the boats broke and the boats ran back downhill with their tons of sand on board to smash into smithereens at the bottom. The massive counterweights – wells with buckets capable of holding 15 tons of water – smashed too.

These, and other vicissitudes, proved the undoing of the canal which was officially closed on 14 November 1891. By 1912 it had been abandoned entirely as a working waterway. Most of it is no longer visible but there are landmarks to be spotted on the Bude Canal Trail, and the stretch beyond Virworthy Mill, below the Lower

Launceston is the only walled town in Cornwall. Once the capital of the county it lost the honour to Bodmin in 1838.

Tamar Lake, is being turned into a nature reserve by the North Cornwall District Council.

Passing through countryside speckled with hamlets, the Tamar is a lonely stream until it reaches Bridgerule in Devon. The county boundary cuts a loop to the west, to make sure that Bridgerule is not in Cornwall, before rejoining the Tamar a mile downstream near Merrifield.

Bridgerule is a village cut in two by the river. Up the hill to the east is its fifteenth-century Church of St Bridget, with a Saxon font, a statue of the saint herself, a carved reredos and a window to the Madonna which was funded by all the Marys in the village.

The river wiggles its way down the valley then, among woodland and pasture. Derril Water flows into it four miles downstream of Bridgerule, and it is swelled by the water of the River Deer near North Tamerton and the River Claw near Tetcott. Other smaller streams tip into it over the next eight

The Tamar's tidal limit is at Gunnislake Weir where sailing boats bob or flop, depending on the water level.

miles or so until the Rivers Ottery and Carey join it approaching the outskirts of Launceston.

This hilltop market town was the capital of Cornwall until 1838, when the more centrally placed Bodmin took on the title. It was William the Conqueror's half brother, Robert de Mortain, who chose the site for the castle from which he would rule Cornwall, and the town grew up around it. Ramparts of a thirteenth-century castle remain, as well as remnants of a twelfth-century Augus-tinian priory. The Church of St Thomas is Norman and boasts the largest font in Cornwall.

By the twelfth century Launceston had become the only walled town in Cornwall. It is still picturesque, with plenty of Georgian houses but only one remaining mediaeval town gate. John Betjeman was moved to write:

Travellers coming out of Devon from Lifton, lift up their hearts at the sight of Launceston.

Betjeman loved Cornwall and, along with the Royal Fine Arts Commission, advised on the reconstruction of the older parts of Launceston after the war. He is buried at St Enodoc at Daymer Bay, a church he immortalised in verse, and even the Launceston Steam Railway, which runs a short section of track in the town, describes itself as being the 'original Betjeman line, Waterloo to Padstow'. It does not go that far now.

'Larnston', as the locals pronounce it, lost its cattle market in 1991 but still has that market town feel to it and is well worth exploring. It is the River Kensey that runs through the town to meet the Tamar to the east and then, between Launceston and Lifton, the River Lyd, fresh from its tumbles over White Lady Falls at Lydford, joins it too. The main Launceston to Tavistock road crosses the river over Greystone Bridge, a superb mediaeval construction with alcoves along its length to allow travellers to tuck in and protect themselves from horses and carts (or today, from articulated lorries). It was an 'indulgence' bridge, funded by the church which persuaded its parishioners to part with money in exchange for the remission of sins: heavenly repentance turned to practical account.

From Launceston southwards the river flows through a deep-sided valley, making an ox-bow through Dunterue

Step back in time at Morwellham Quay where the quayside buildings have been turned into a living museum.

Up to a dozen vessels could be moored at Morwellham Quay in its heyday.

The viaduct over the Tamar at Calstock is symbolic of the triumph of railway over river. Cargoes that were once transported by water moved to the railway and Calstock had to look for a different way of earning its living.

Wood where another major tributary, the River Inny, flows into it. Fish abound in these waters and salmon rest in the deep, oak-shadowed pools on their way upriver.

The combined force of all these waters then reaches Gunnislake, a town dating mainly from the eighteenth and nineteenth centuries when the local mines yielded tin, copper and wolfram, from which came tungsten. The seven-arched bridge over the Tamar here dates from the fourteenth century. The weir below Gunnislake marks the upstream limit of tidal waters. A mile downstream from the weir is Morwellham Quay, once a riverside port and now 'The Living Past – an unforgettable experience of learning and enjoyment for all ages'.

At one time a dozen 300-ton vessels could moor here to take on copper, arsenic and manganese, and to unload limestone, timber and coal. By 1868 it was 'the greatest copper port in Queen Victoria's Empire'; by 1900 it was aban-doned. Run by the Morwellham Trust, the Quay is now open all year round to give a taste of what things were like in the port's heyday, as well as offering the customary carriage rides, new-born farm animals and the like. More pertinent are the rides 'deep into an ancient copper mine' with its 'giant water-wheel pumping away in the dark'. It is important that we know what went on in the past when people and country-side worked hand in hand, but I cannot help wondering if one day the whole thing will become little more than a spectator sport.

The clue as to the demise of these river ports lies at Gunnislake: the terminus of the Tamar Valley Railway which runs the fourteen miles down to Plymouth. It is a beautiful line but one which saw off the river competition. Calstock was a river port, too, handling granite, paper, copper and bricks. The railway crosses the Tamar Valley high above Calstock on a spectacular viaduct, symbolic of its triumph over the water. Now Calstock has turned to growing strawberries, gooseberries and cherries: from stone to stone fruit.

The quays are still used, but only by day-trippers from Plymouth who come up the Tamar by pleasure boat. They enjoy the attractive town, which clings to the hillside, and the discerning amongst them also take in Cotehele House with its quay and mill, just across the loop of the river.

Cotehele is owned by the National Trust, who have also done their bit to show what went on when the quayside (now restored) was a bustling port. The sailing barge *Shamrock*, dating from 1899, has also been restored and is moored on the quay. Time was when the river bristled with these barges, taking copper and tin down to Plymouth and Devonport and bringing back coal and limestone for the lime-kilns at Morwellham.

The fully restored eighteenth-century watermill at Cotehele still grinds corn on occasions but it is the house, dating from the fourteenth to the seventeenth centuries, that is more handsome. Here lived the Edgecumbe family until the house was handed over to the National Trust in 1947. The majority of the house is Tudor and the surrounding gardens that run down to the river are justly famous.

Towering over the Tamar is the 'Chapel on the Cliff'. This 70-foot-high building was built by Sir Richard Edgecumbe in gratitude for his escape from the forces of Richard III. Having declared his allegiance to the future Henry VII in 1485, he was attacked by Richard's followers and threw his cap, weighted by a stone, into the river. When they saw it his pursuers assumed he had leapt to his death and called off the search. Later he fought at the battle of Bosworth Field and was knighted by his new monarch.

The river widens gradually now until it becomes an estuary. At Cargreen there was once a ferry and just round the corner is a smaller estuary that leads into the Tamar. This is known as Kingsmill Lake and its mud flats in winter are home to avocets, those black and white waders

with upturned bills that are rare enough to have become the symbol of the Royal Society for the Protection of Birds. There are green sandpipers, black-tailed godwits and spotted redshanks here, too.

Just opposite Kingsmill Lake the Tamar is joined by the River Tavy for the last leg of its journey under Isambard Kingdom Brunel's famous railway bridge that links Plymouth with Saltash. Brunel was born in 1806, the son of Sir Marc Brunel, the French-born engineer who was responsible for

Unloading barges at Cotehele was a mechanised business, even in the 1860s.

The quay at Cotehele is now managed by the National Trust. The sailing barge Shamrock *is berthed here and the buildings have been restored.*

the first tunnel underneath the River Thames. The son would go on to become Britain's most famous civil, marine and mechanical engineer of Victorian times. When he was only twenty-three Isambard designed the Clifton Suspension Bridge, which was not actually completed until five years after his death. In 1833 he became engineer to the Great Western Railway and designed the Saltash Bridge, also known as the Royal Albert Bridge. This one was completed in the year of his death: 1859. His name, and the date, are picked out in white letters on the end. At least he was able to supervise the construction before he died. As the great girders were raised into position, Brunel signalled them into place from the central pier by waving flags.

A suspension bridge to take motor traffic now runs alongside the railway bridge to the south. It was opened in 1961, 102 years after Brunel's master-piece. Devon is to the east of the estuary and Cornwall to the west – the bridges link the two counties, and between Plymouth and Launceston there are only four points at which the Tamar can be crossed.

Saltash is a fishing port built on a steep hill above the estuary and has a seventeenth-century guildhall built on granite pillars. It waited a long time to be within shopping distance of Plymouth, just over the water. Daniel Defoe found that crossing the river from Plymouth to Saltash was a chancy affair in the early eighteenth century:

The Tamar here is very wide, and the ferry boats bad, so that I thought myself well escaped, when I got safe on shore in Cornwall.

A ferry crossing still operates between Torpoint, on the western bank of the Tamar, and Devonport, the part of Plymouth that runs alongside the channel known as Hamoaze.

The centre of Plymouth, the largest city in the west country, was almost totally destroyed in the Second World War but has since been rebuilt. On the edges of the town fragments of history remain. Look at the Barbican (nothing like London's), which gives a real flavour of old Plymouth. Here are quayside pubs and ship's chandlers and, yes, the odd antique shop. When I say that the fish and chips here are terrific I mean it as a compliment. Fish always tastes better when there is a whiff of salt in the air.

There is a whiff of history in the air, too. The Phoenicians came to trade in tin, and Romans and Saxons settled

John Smeaton's Tower was the third Eddystone Lighthouse and the first to be built of stone. It stood its ground from 1759 to 1882 until undermined by the sea. Now it stands on Plymouth Hoe as a memorial to its clockmaker designer.

here. It is events from Elizabethan times, however, that we know most about from our schooldays. Sir Walter Raleigh sailed from here, as did Sir John Hawkins, Martin Frobisher and Sir Francis Drake, who calmly finished his game of bowls on Plymouth Hoe before going out to polish off the Spanish Armada in 1588. Drake was probably aware that the tides were not right at that point in his game, and that he might as well win both contests.

The Pilgrim Fathers sailed from Plymouth to America in the *Mayflower* in 1620, and Captain James Cook left here for his circumnavigation of the world in 1772. This was just 194 years before Francis Chichester did the same

One man who left his mark on the English river was Isambard Kingdom Brunel. The Saltash Bridge bears the date 1859 and carries what was the Great Western Railway over the Tamar from Devon to Cornwall.

on his own in a little boat called *Gypsy Moth IV*, between 1966 and 1967.

Now Plymouth is an industrial and naval city but you can still look out to sea from Plymouth Hoe beside a statue of Sir Francis Drake. Not far from the Armada Memorial, erected to mark the tercentenary of his victory, and the Naval War Memorial, Drake gazes across Plymouth Sound where the waters of the Tamar join those of the River Plym. Three miles long and three miles wide, the Sound covers 4500 acres at high tide.

Apart from being an important naval base, the Sound is also a great nature reserve. This is thanks to the shelter provided by the surrounding headlands and the protection from severe seas by the Plymouth Breakwater, a mile-long barrier two miles out to sea. Many birds overwinter in the Sound and gulls in particular enjoy the rich pickings of sewage

On Plymouth Hoe is a statue of the man who was playing bowls here when he received news of the Spanish Armada – Sir Francis Drake.

The waters of Plymouth Sound – entry point of the Tamar into the sea. Past Drake's Island the river flows with the ferries to foreign parts.

outfalls. Oystercatchers, turnstones and purple sandpipers pick over the mudflats on the shoreline. Slavonian grebes, goosanders and red-breasted mergansers fish farther out. Wild flowers enjoy the coast conditions, too – maidenhair fern, Plymouth thistle and eryngium among them. There are rich rewards around here for anyone with a pair of binoculars and an interest in natural history.

The tide flows on past Drake's Island, a fort and one-time prison, into the English Channel. From here, in the wake of the Pilgrim Fathers, it makes its way into the Atlantic Ocean.

The Severn

Height at source: 2000 feet
Length: 220 miles
Runs from Bryn-Cras, Plynlimon, to Bristol

On Wenlock Edge the wood's in trouble;
His forest fleece the Wrekin heaves;
The gale, it plies the saplings double,
And thick on Severn snow the leaves.

from *A Shropshire Lad* by A. E. Houseman, 1896

Were it not for the fact that the River Severn rises in Wales, it would be the longest river in England, but then as it can claim to being the longest river in Britain it is hardly likely to care. It rises high up on Bryn-Cras, one of the peaks of Pumlumon Fawr (known to the English as Plynlimon), about fifteen miles to the east of Aberystwyth. In Wales the river is known as Afon Hafren, and during the first fifteen miles of its life tumbles from a height of 2000 feet to 500 feet. The acrobatics dispensed with, its flow thereafter is more sedate.

The Severn is a mixture of the romantic and the practical. On the romantic side it is said to have been named after the nymph Sabrina who died within its waters, and on the practical side it provides water for six million of the British population in such towns and cities as Birmingham, Worcester, Gloucester, Wolverhampton and Bristol. I drink it regularly in Birmingham and you can taste the peaty richness.

Reservoirs on the Rivers Clywedog and Vyrnwy are used both to top up the flow of the Severn in summer and ensure a continuation of domestic water supply. Lake Vyrnwy is the supplier of Liverpool's water.

Through the Hafren Forest, the river flows down to Llanidloes where it

Sabrina, goddess of the River Severn, reclining in a bower in Quarry Park, Shrewsbury. Sabrina was a nymph who supposedly perished in the waters of the river.

is swollen by the Rivers Dulas and Clywedog, and then it heads north-eastwards to Newtown, taking on the waters of the Trannon and the Carno. Past Welshpool, having been joined by the River Camlad (the only river to flow from England into Wales), the Severn finally reaches England at the point where it meets the River Vyrnwy.

The two unite among green fields near Melverley, whose ancient black and white church is made of timber, and then the enlarged river snakes across more meadows towards Shrawardine. There was a Norman castle here, but as a stronghold of the King in the Civil War it fell after a five-day siege in 1645 and suffered the ulti-mate indignity of being dismantled and used to repair Shrewsbury Castle. Nowadays Shrawardine Pool offers more interest – 40 acres of water that act as a sanctuary for rare birds.

Shortly after flowing under Montford Bridge, built by Thomas Telford in 1790 and responsible for enhancing his reputation, the Severn takes on the River Perry and then glides towards its first English town, Shrewsbury. But pause for a moment at Montford Bridge to reflect on the fact that it was here, in 1283, that David, the last Welsh Prince of Wales, was handed to the English in chains. He was executed as a traitor by Edward I on 3 October of that year.

And so to Shrewsbury, the county town of Shropshire. It is made almost an island by a loop in the Severn and owes its foundation to the inhabitants of nearby Wroxeter who, on the depar-ture of the Roman legions in the fifth century, needed a site that was more easily defended. The Normans built a castle there, which was added to over the centuries and eventually turned into a private house for Sir William Pulteney by Thomas Telford.

Despite the demolition of many old buildings over the last century, Shrewsbury still has plenty to recom-mend it – black and white Elizabethan buildings, including Abbots House which dates from 1450, and the twelfth-century St Mary's Church. It was from a rope tied to the spire of this church that a rash youth by the name of Cadman tried to cross the River Severn in 1739. As his wife below collected the coppers he plunged to his death. A plaque on the wall of the tower commemorates his sad folly in rhyme.

Other notables are remembered in Shrewsbury: Charles Dickens, Paganini and Jenny Lind all stayed at the Lion Hotel, and Charles Darwin went to Shrewsbury School. In the latter part of the twentieth century, Shrewsbury became famous for its gardens in the

The church at Melverley is black and white, one of only two churches in Shropshire to be built of timber – solid English oak – at the turn of the fourteenth century.

Dawn on Shrawardine Pool where forty acres of water act as a refuge for wildfowl.

Dingle and the Quarry Park (which originally provided the red stone from which the old town was built), and for its Flower Show. The raised horticultural profile was due mainly to the work of Percy Thrower who was Parks Superintendent from 1946 to 1974, and also the most famous of television gardeners. The river flows around the Quarry, and one of the best ways of looking at the two bridges that span the Severn in Shrewsbury – the English Bridge of 1769, and the Welsh Bridge of 1791 – is by rowing boat.

To leave the town the river flows under the English Bridge and winds southwards to take on the River Tern near the village of Atcham. There are two more bridges across the Severn here – the seven-arched beauty was built in the same year and by the same man who built the English Bridge – John Gwynne. The other bridge dates from 1929, and across the road is the

The English Bridge at Shrewsbury, under which the River Severn flows as it leaves the town. It was built in 1769 by John Gwynne.

gateway to Attingham Park, built for the first Lord Berwick with grounds laid out by Humphry Repton. It is now in the hands of the National Trust. The church at Atcham is the only one in the country dedicated to St Eata (died 686), Bishop of Hexham. It was built of stone taken from the ruins of the Roman Viroconium, round the next bend in the river, known today as Wroxeter.

As Viroconium, Wroxeter was the fourth largest Roman town in Britain. Now it is a village but remnants of those earlier legions remain. The old Roman road peters out at the river. Parts of the church here were built by the Saxons who also used Roman remains. There are other relics on view, including pillars of a Roman bridge that once crossed the Severn.

In those days the river was an important navigation channel, and in the thirteenth century paving stones

The Dingle in Shrewsbury is a fine testimony to the man who put it on the map: Percy Thrower, the man they called 'England's Head Gardener'.

were being taken up as far as Shrewsbury on barges. In the seventeenth century navigability extended from Welshpool to Bristol and both passengers and cargo were carried on barges and on trows – shallow-draught boats with collapsible masts capable of coping with bridges and variations in water depth. Trows were anything up to 50 feet long and could carry up to 80 tons. When the sails could not be used for power, bow-hauliers stepped in – teams of men who dragged the barges and trows on the river. It cost a merchant 10 shillings to have his cargo taken downstream from Shrewsbury to Bristol, and 15 shillings to have it taken upstream from Bristol to Shrewsbury. Not for nothing was the Severn described as the greatest of England's trading rivers and the second busiest river in Europe.

Past Eyton on Severn the river loops round Cressage, a Saxon settlement which is recorded in the Domesday Book as having fishing rights on the river. The Severn is still plentiful in fish today. Most salmon are caught further downstream, but trout are caught in some of its tributaries and in the upstream waters along with bream, chub, barbel, roach, dace, perch, gudgeon and pike. The introduced zander is also building up. Once the Severn was prized as the best river for lampreys – parasitic eel-like creatures that fasten themselves to other fish for sustenance. So highly were they regarded as a delicacy that Henry I is reputed to have died from eating more of them than was good for him.

The translation of Cressage is 'Christ's Oak' – a meeting place for early Christians before their church was built. Telford's wooden bridge, which used to cross the river here, has now been replaced by one made of ferro-concrete. Where once timber held sway in worship and in river-crossing the greater durability of iron and stone has triumphed.

There is proof of this as the river glides between the towering peak of

Coalbrookdale is where coke was first used in the smelting of iron, and today its power station clouds the sky.

the Wrekin and the line of hills known as Wenlock Edge past the remains of Buildwas Abbey. In spite of the dissolution damage, much of the Abbey still stands by the river where the monks were granted loading facilities for their barges and where they also dipped their sheep. One of Telford's iron bridges survives here, too, but it is just after the modern cooling towers of a power station that the most famous bridge stretches over the Severn Gorge – *the* Ironbridge that gave its name to the town.

Cast in adjacent Coalbrookdale by Abraham Darby III, the bridge was opened on 1 January 1781. It was the first iron bridge in the world and held together, not by rivets, but by carpentry joints and wedges. Until the 1930s the 100-foot arch carried traffic; now it carries pedestrians across the gorge that was formed as a result of flooding after the Ice Age. The raging waters revealed seams of coal, iron-stone and limestone which were to become the basis of the economy for this valley, often referred to as the cradle of the Industrial Revolution.

It was in Coalbrookdale, just a mile north-west of the Ironbridge, that Abraham Darby I discovered how to use coke in the smelting of iron in 1709. His son and grandson continued to develop the business and the gorge belched with smoke and became a thriving community. The River Severn played a crucial part in the success of the iron industry, providing a cheap means of transporting raw materials, iron and coal from Bristol and

Bridgnorth – a town split into two parts: High Town and Low Town.

Gloucester. The first iron boat was launched near here, and the first iron railway lines were made in Coalbrookdale. The Ironbridge Gorge Museum Trust now safeguards the area where there is still plenty of evidence of the town's original talents. Ironbridge's golden years lasted about a century. They eventually declined due to the opening up of the canal network that took trade to the Black Country where there were greater supplies of iron and coal. Today Georgian cottages still cling to the steep sides of the valley and landslips are not unknown.

A bottle-oven at Coalport where fine china was manufactured until 1926 when the firm moved to Staffordshire.

126

In 1880 the river was totally blocked by subsidence at Buildwas.

Just across the Severn to the south is activity of a more pastoral nature. Benthall Edge Wood is an ancient oak and lime woodland and is rich in plant and animal life. Here are butterfly orchids, herb paris, wild service trees and other delights.

They are the sort of flowers to be found in the designs on Coalport china, manufactured barely two miles downriver from the mid-eighteenth century until 1926 when the firm moved to Staffordshire. Now the kilns and potteries are a museum, showing off the porcelain china for which the firm was famous in the days before it was taken over by Wedgwood.

Southwards now, with woodland on its high-rise banks, the river has only half a dozen miles to travel to Bridgnorth. It is joined by the River Worfe before it slices clean through the town; a town with two distinct halves. Above the river on sandstone cliffs is High Town, and by the riverside is Low Town. A cliff railway and a six-arched road bridge connect the two parts of this market town which has the remains of a Norman castle keep that leans even more than the Tower of Pisa. There is plenty to marvel at architecturally in Bridgnorth, and High Town offers great views of the River Severn gliding by below.

The caves in the cliff were once used to store the Cave Ale for which Bridgnorth was famous, and the Church of St Mary Magdalene – Italianate in style – was built by

Upper Arley – where the railway line crosses the river and rods come into play.

Thomas Telford (in this case a bridge to heaven).

From Bridgnorth to Kidderminster, about sixteen miles away, runs the Severn Valley Railway, a steam locomotive line that follows the river for much of its course. It is a spectacular run in delightful scenery. Past Quatford on its east bank, where the Danes camped and the Normans built a church, and Chelmarsh to the west – an unspoilt village with timbered cottages and a fourteenth-century church – the river and the railway run due south until the line crosses the water on Victoria Bridge near Upper Arley. Twice as long as Darby's Ironbridge, this bridge was built by Sir John Fowler, who designed the Forth Bridge in Scotland, and designed by Thomas Telford. If you are wondering why Telford did so much in this neck of the woods it is all down to his being appointed Surveyor of Public

Works for Shropshire in 1787. A good investment on their part.

The Severn now leaves Shropshire and crosses the county boundary into Hereford and Worcester. At Bewdley it passes under another Telford Bridge which was built to replace the one that was swept away by the great flood of 1795. Bewdley, situated to the west of the larger Kidderminster, has a strange history. Once it was used by fugitives from the two counties of Shropshire and Worcestershire because it was regarded as neutral territory. This state of affairs continued until the town was declared as belonging to Worcestershire in 1544. It occupies a hill on the side of the river.

Pleasure boats and skiffs ply the waters that once took commercial traffic, and the seventeenth and eighteenth-century houses are echoes of Bewdley's prosperous past as a river port. Both the Bewdley Museum and the station on the Severn Valley Line whisk back in time those keen on escaping the modern world.

One of Bewdley's greatest glories today is Wyre Forest on its western side. Hundreds of acres of forest offer a multitude of different habitats that are under the care of the Nature Conservancy Council, the Forestry Commission and Worcestershire Nature Conservancy Trust. Here are goldcrests and firecrests, the shy hawfinch, fallow deer, rare butterflies, dragonflies and damsel flies. The pure waters of Dowles Brooke, that runs through the forest before joining the

Thomas Telford's bridge over the Severn at Bewdley, built in 1795.

The station at Bewdley has been lovingly preserved and allows escapists to step back into an age when steam ruled on the railway.

Severn at Dowles, support salmon, stone loach, trout, bullhead and fresh-water crayfish. The Severn here boasts the rare club-tailed dragonfly, as well as that prince among mammals, the otter.

Once the otter was plentiful in Britain – a population of 20,000 was estimated in 1950. By 1980 numbers in England had been reduced by ninety-four per cent due to habitat destruction and river pollution. Thanks to renewed efforts by conservation organisations, the banning of many poisonous agri-cultural chemicals and the restoration of riverbank vegetation, the otters are building up in numbers. They are moving out from strongholds in Wales, Scotland and the West Country, and recent sightings have been made at several places on the Severn.

Past Ribbesford Woods to the south of Bewdley, the Severn glides through Stourport-on-Severn. Until the coming

Worcester is an ancient town with a fine legacy of architecture, from mediaeval to Georgian and Victorian. A fine stone bridge across the Severn was built by John Gwynne between 1771 and 1780 and subsequently enlarged.

From Stourport downstream the River Severn is navigable at all times, due to weirs and locks which have been built to maintain water levels. Shrawley Wood rises above the western river bank south of Stourport and is the best example of a lime wood in the West Midlands. A large pool has been dammed to encourage dragonflies and damsel flies, including the rare hawker, and there are masses of wildflowers and breeding birds.

Through locks and a weir at Holt Fleet, the river runs by Grimley – the site of a Roman fort – and into the city of Worcester. The Romans passed through it on their way from Glevum (Gloucester) to Salinae (Droitwich) for their salt.

An example of Upton-on-Severn's historic architecture – Ye Olde Anchor Inn, built in 1601.

of the Staffordshire and Worcestershire Canal in 1771, this was a sleepy village. Then, in the late eighteenth century, it became the 'Venice of the Midlands' where the canal, the River Severn and the River Stour all met. For a time it was the busiest inland port in the Midlands, after Birmingham, but now all the canal carries is pleasure craft.

The canal was intended to link the rivers Trent and Severn, joining the Severn at Bewdley. But Bewdley wanted none of it, and the canal's builder, James Brindley, took it to Stourmouth instead – a decision that has left the present town of Stourport with a legacy of fine buildings. Like so many enterprises connected with waterways, this one was successful for about a century. Then the arrival of the railway and the opening of the Birmingham and Worcester Canal diverted the traffic in other directions.

Stourport's designation as a 'resort of people of fashion' continued until this century, when Birmingham folk still considered it as a place to go for weekend relaxation.

Thanks to the fact that Cromwell knocked it about a bit in the Civil War, Worcester suffered greatly in the seventeenth century but there are still plenty of old bits that inspire. The cathedral stands on a site just above the river where a wooden settlement was built in the seventh century. The cathedral was built between 1084 and 1375, and lying in the centre of a stupendous knave is the tomb of King John who died in 1216. Prince Arthur, brother of Henry VII, is also buried here.

The early Georgian Guildhall and a rich assortment of mediaeval houses make for fascinating exploration, and Worcester is remembered by many as the birthplace of Sir Edward Elgar. The cottage at Lower Broadheath, in which he was born in 1857, is a place of manuscripts, scores, photographs and press clippings, and it opens at assorted times during the year. Elgar loved the Severn. When he moved to London he named his house 'Severn House', and late in life he composed a work known as the 'Severn Suite'.

The site of the Battle of Worcester of 1651 is to the south of the city, and King Charles House in New Street is where Charles II sheltered briefly after defeat and hurried out of the back door to escape his Parliamentarian enemies. 'Love God, honour ye King', it says over the lintel.

The river plays a part in sporting activities at Worcester – the racecourse is on the banks of the Severn, and the river regularly floods the county cricket ground. Flood meadows, or hams, are an important outlet for rising

Odda's Chapel, near Deerhurst, was built in 1056 and still survives.

tides on the Severn, though even these cannot always alleviate disasters. In 1795, sixteen bridges in Shropshire were demolished by flood waters. Today the area south of Worcester is still prone to flooding, though £25 million is being spent on flood defences between the city of Gloucester and Avonmouth.

The river offers the likes of pike, chub, dace, roach, bream, salmon and trout to fishermen at Worcester. But it is for Royal Worcester porcelain, first manufactured in 1751, and Worcester sauce, manufactured in 1830 to the

By a bend in the River Severn is Ashleworth with its mediaeval tithe barn.

recipe of the Governor of Bengal who stayed at Worcester, that the city is most famous. The glove industry still thrives, and the Birmingham and Worcester Canal which joins the Severn here was once a main artery of the area's commerce.

The Severn divides around an island at Diglis, with a weir to one side, and shortly afterwards is reinforced by the River Teme. A new bridge spans the river just south of the confluence, carrying the A422 across the water. A viewing platform has been built and there are panels describing the history of the Battle of Worcester. Nowadays the National Rivers Authority is encouraging bridge designers to incorporate bird nesting areas into their bridges to provide habitats for dippers, spotted flycatchers and wagtails. Even Telford never did that.

Southwards now past Kempsey and Severn Stoke, the river meanders through meadows that offer views to the west of the Malvern Hills, barely five miles away, and then glides through Upton upon Severn, where

Gloucester lasted longer as an inland port than most other river towns. Only in the 1970s did river traffic dwindle to a standstill.

river craft can be hired to take you as far away as Evesham. The bridge across the river is modern, but much of the architecture is antique. There are Georgian houses by the river, and the White Lion Inn featured in Henry Fielding's *Tom Jones*, but the four-teenth-century bell tower (known locally as the 'Pepperpot') is Upton's most famous landmark. The battle of Upton Bridge in the Civil War destroyed the rest of the church and many local buildings. There are delightful riverside walks at Upton upon Severn. The land round here is susceptible to flooding but the raising of road levels has hopefully eased the situation for future inhabitants.

Downstream, past Ripple, the site of the last Royalist victory in the Civil War, the Queenhill Viaduct takes the M50 motorway across the river which then flows through meadows to Tewkesbury. It joins the Avon here (see the chapter on that river for details of Tewkesbury) and then, much fatter, and fuller and wider, it sails into Gloucestershire.

The village of Deerhurst may look tiny on the map but it was here that King Edmund and King Cnut met in 1016 to redraw the boundary between the Saxons and the Danes. Its priory church is still in use and can lay claim to being one of the oldest churches in Britain. Odda's Chapel, attached to the house nearby, dates from 1056. Who was Odda? A friend of Edward the Confessor who erected the chapel to the memory of his brother.

The river has a pronounced bend at

Sharpness juts out into the Severn Estuary between Slimbridge and Berkeley; its docks and boatyards are hugely popular with artists and holiday sketchers.

Ashleworth, where once there was a quay and where a few limestone mediaeval buildings remain, and then the Severn comes to Gloucester.

The city owes its existence to the river. The Roman fort of Glevum guarded this lowest crossing point on the Severn, and a fortified harbour was built here in preparation for the invasion of Wales in the first century AD. There are still remnants of the Romans on view, and plenty of mediaeval buildings, too. But the pride and joy of Gloucester is its cathedral, built between 1089 and 1260, and remodelled in the fourteenth century so that the tomb of Edward II could be accommodated. With its early examples of Perpendicular architecture, and an east window of stained glass, second in size only to York Minster, the cathedral is a great attraction.

One of Gloucester's less attractive facets is its effluent which reduces the quality of the Severn's water below the city. A new treatment plant planned for the turn of the century should do much to improve things. In spite of the impurities, 3000 salmon are caught commercially between Gloucester and Avonmouth, and around 1000 are caught by rod on the rest of the river each year. But elvers (young eels) are not as plentiful as they were and efforts are being made to replenish stocks so that they can hold their own with the sturgeon, lampern and twaite shad that survive in the tidal stretches of river below Gloucester.

With the building of the Gloucester and Sharpness Canal in 1827, the city had a sixteen-mile-long commercial link with the Severn Estuary that enabled ships of up to 1000 tons to avoid being restricted by the tides. Its construction ensured Gloucester's success as an inland port. Until the mid 1960s, industrial water traffic used Gloucester Harbour, and oil traffic continued until the late 1970s when pipelines and road haulage became the preferred means of transport. Today commerce in the docks is of the kind to which we have become accustomed: 'turning historical warehouses to exciting new uses', to quote the brochure. Even Merchant's Quay has become 'an exciting new shopping pavilion'. Exciting to whom?

The River Severn is tidal below Gloucester, and south of the city it widens dramatically, leaving great areas of mudflat and sandbank at low tide.

Minsterworth, on the north bank of the Severn just below Gloucester, is a fine place to observe the phenomenon known as the Severn Bore. Early spring and late summer tides vary in height by as much as 40 feet between high and low tide, and it is this, coupled with the dramatic narrowing of the estuary and a rising of the riverbed at Awre, that produce a bottleneck and a build-up of incoming tide that can sometimes rush upstream in a wave as high as 6 feet. Travelling at around ten miles per hour, this tidal wave makes its way upstream as far as Gloucester, where twin weirs dissipate its power. The National Rivers Authority produces timetables which show the dates when the bore is likely to be at its most spectacular and locals turn out in force to watch the most interesting bore in Britain rolling up the Severn.

Downstream at Framilode the Stroudwater Canal, which linked the Severn with the Thames, once connected with the river, but now only short sections of it can be traced across the countryside. The River Frome runs alongside it and at Framilode pours out into the Severn.

Making a great loop around Arlingham, the river bank exposes fossil-bearing jurassic limestone at Garden Cliff, and at nearby Westbury-on-Severn are the earliest surviving Dutch-style water gardens in Britain. Westbury Court Gardens date from the seventeenth century and have been restored to their former glory. The river then loops past Newnham, nestling in

Pay your toll and cross the estuary by the Severn Bridge. Until 1966 a ferry made the journey even more precarious.

the shadow of the Forest of Dean, and Bullo Pill, a tidal creek where once there was a wet dock for the exporting of Forest of Dean coal.

My favourite village on this stretch of the river is Frampton on Severn, with its huge village green decorated with three large ponds and a cricket pitch, and the small but perfectly formed house of Frampton Court, dating from 1731. In Frampton Manor, just across the green, Henry II's 'Fair Rosamund' is reputed to have been born. Her descendants, the Clifford family, have lived in Frampton for around 800 years, and both houses and gardens can be visited by appointment.

From here downstream the Severn Estuary is a Site of Special Scientific Interest that is recognised as an internationally important wetland habitat, and it is just below Frampton on Severn that the Wildfowl and Wetlands Trust has its reserve at Slimbridge. Founded in 1946 by Sir Peter Scott, its natural wetlands are home to white-fronted geese, all manner of ducks and waterfowl and an enormous flock of Bewick swans. I sat with Peter Scott one winter in his study that overlooked 'Swan Lake' and watched these beauties gliding across the water. Behind him was a painting of them, half finished. White feathers and golden beaks stood out against an azure sky. I will never forget it.

On the south bank of the estuary now is the Vale of Berkeley, backed up by the Cotswold Hills, and to the north is the Forest of Dean. After a narrowing between Sharpness and Lydney, the main Forest of Dean port in the eighteenth century, the estuary widens within a stone's throw of Berkeley Castle. This is England's oldest inhabited castle dating from 1153, and the Berkeley family still lives here.

Ten miles downstream the river flows under the famous Severn Bridge. Until 1966 the only way to cross the estuary above water level was by ferry from Aust, something that had been going on since pre-Roman times. In 1886 the railway tunnel under the estuary was completed, making it the longest railway tunnel in Britain, and now the toll bridge links England with Wales. Soon there will be yet another bridge below the existing one – work is already underway.

Diggers will no doubt discover more remains of prehistoric animals that lie within the cliffs of Aust; remains that have been embedded in the clay and limestone of the Westbury Beds for around 200 million years.

Washing away a few more bones each year, the Severn, joined by the River Wye just below the bridge, surges in a great, wide, grey-brown torrent of muddy fluid into the Bristol Channel.

Few mill-wheels now turn on the English river, but alternative sources of power are in evidence. Would Turner have set up his easel near Oldbury for this?

The Avon

Height at source: 600 feet
Length: 75 miles
Runs from Naseby to Tewkesbury

. . . such waters as these are for dreaming on in the full flush of summer, for catching the moods of summer skies, or doubling the splendour of autumn woods; for reflecting the ruddy glow of brick bridges, the moist and lichen-covered walls of old brick mills.

A.G. Bradley in *The Rivers and Streams of England,* 1909

A monument near Naseby commemorates the battle of 1645 when Charles I lost his crown to Cromwell. The Avon rises a strenuous stones-throw from the battleground.

Close your eyes, engage your imagination and listen carefully at the source of the Warwickshire Avon. On a still day you may hear the distant sounds of clashing steel, whinnying horses and men at war, for the Avon rises at Naseby in Northamptonshire where, on 14 June 1645, Oliver Cromwell and the Parliamentarians defeated Charles I. Five thousand men were injured, a thousand lost their lives, and the King lost his crown.

The battlefield lies about a mile north of Naseby and the source of the river is a well in the garden of Manor Farm just opposite the church. From here it flows under the road and through the cellars of the Fitzgerald Arms, named after the family who were Lords of the Manor during the Enclosure Acts. Over a century ago, this infant river was diverted through the mouth of a plaster swan which spurted into an ornamental pool. But the proud bird was too great a temptation for the local lads and fell victim to a spot of poaching.

From this unusual source, the river flows through Naseby, then snakes its way through green meadows to the first Welford on the Avon. There is another one later on.

Here the river plays nip and tuck with the Grand Union Canal. The Wharf House Hotel, once the George Inn, has a castellated top and sits next to the road where it crosses the river.

The old boatyard here has become a smart marina where narrow-boats can be hired, or simply watched chugging to and fro while you sample a pint of Ansells bitter.

The flow becomes more powerful now, as befits a river that for the next ten or twelve miles will divide the counties of Northamptonshire and Leicestershire. The Avon is not an especially clean river, but what it lacks in purity it makes up for in power. The water is mighty enough to have once turned the wheels of Bosworth and Kilworth Mills. Now it flows on through Stanford Reservoir until it reaches Stanford Hall. This impressive William and Mary mansion stands among sweeping parkland and, like all stately homes today, has to compete for its customers. There are displays of costumes and motorcycles and an intriguing curio: a replica of Percy Pilcher's flying machine.

How could you not have heard of Percy Pilcher, the pioneering aviator? As a friend of the Verney Caves who lived at Stanford Hall, he came to stay and to try out his machines – kite-like structures of bamboo, wire and cotton sheets. Alas, in his fourth model, *The Hawk*, he crash-landed and was killed a few hundred yards from the Avon in 1899. A monument marks the spot across the river from the Hall. It was erected by the Royal Aeronautical Society. Poor Percy.

Over the next few miles the river flows towards Rugby. It goes under the M1, with its invasive roar, and a mile further on under Watling Street, that

Beyond Rugby, at Little Lawford, a bridleway crosses the Avon by bridge but motorists must splash through the ford. The mill, mentioned in the Domesday Book, still stands.

straight-as-a-die Roman road from Canterbury to Chester which now is burdened with the name of A5(T).

At Dow Bridge, where the stone bridge of 1232 is joined by its replacement – a single-span structure, the River Avon enters the county of Warwickshire. 'Shakespeare's County' proclaim signs on the county borders.

Clifton upon Dunsmore is the next village, notable as the birthplace of Lawrence Sheriff. When he died in 1567, this successful London grocer left a legacy for the founding of a grammar school in the nearby town. It

eventually became a public school, famous for a game played with an oval ball, and for a fictional pupil by the name of Tom Brown. Mr Sheriff was the man behind Rugby.

Dr Arnold, the famous headmaster of Rugby School from 1828 to 1842, can have the first and last word on Rugby town, which the river skirts to the north. He wrote: 'It stands on rising ground between which and the Ural Mountains, there is nothing to intercept the wind.'

Having been joined by the River Swift it is through Newbould on Avon that the Avon flows in its effort to avoid Rugby. Having passed under the Oxford Canal outside Clifton upon Dunsmore, the Avon comes close to it now before they part for ever.

Footbridges cross and recross the river here, and there is a long footbridge across the flood meadows. At the next village of Little Lawford, cars must splash through a ford; only pedestrians and those on horseback can use the footbridge. Then the river flows on to Kings Newnham where once the saline springs of Newnham Regis promised a spa town to rival Leamington. Two hundred years ago the springs were much visited and greatly revered, but the spa town never happened and the springs have vanished without trace. Wolston and Brandon are divided by the river, and Wolston Mill, once powered by the Avon's water, is now no more than a pile of rubble. There is only one more village between here and Coventry, and that is Ryton-on-Dunsmore. Until recently the most famous thing about this village, which is sliced in half by the A45, was that the husband of Lady Godiva, Earl Leofric, had given the place to the priory of Coventry in 1043. Now, to gardeners like me, it is known as the seat of the organic gardening movement – the Henry Doubleday Research Association is based here.

Avoiding Coventry, the Avon snakes away to the south towards the farmer's mecca – Stoneleigh and the National Agricultural Centre, home of the Royal Show. When Charles Showell ventured down the lane to Stoneleigh at the turn of the century he remarked that 'there is not a more romantic one in all Warwickshire'. Stoneleigh is still a picturesque English village with a green and sixteenth-century almshouses in warm sandstone. They were built by Alice Leigh, daughter of the Lord Mayor of London at the time of Elizabeth I's coronation.

The river that flows through the centre of the village is not the Avon but the Sowe, which joins the Avon some little way downstream where the two then flow as the Avon past the National Agricultural Centre and Stoneleigh Abbey, a Cistercian Community founded by Henry II in 1154. Part of the original building survives, but more dates from the seventeenth, eighteenth and nineteenth centuries. Home to the Leigh family since 1651, it is soon to become a hotel and golf complex. *Sic transit gloria mundi.*

Round a wooded hill, then passing the tiny village of Ashow, the river runs deep through reeds alongside the church. It is a church that shows evidence of Sunday archery practice, as ordained by Edward III in 1363.

When Charles Showell penned 'Shakespeare's Avon' in 1901 the mill at Wolston was still working. Now it is a total ruin.

Like a strand of silver thread the Avon winds between rolling hills towards Warwick now. Just north of the town it cascades over the weir at Guy's Cliffe.

The weir belongs to the 'Saxon Mill', said to date from around the ninth century. Nowadays it is a restaurant and nestles among the trees looking like some Tyrolean wayside inn in an Ivor Novello musical. That is more than can be said for Guy's Cliffe House just downriver of the mill. A Palladian mansion built in 1751 it is now a ruin surrounded by ever-encroaching vegetation threatening at every minute to swallow it up. The Guy in question is Guy of Warwick who, having defended the Saxon cause against the Danes on his return to Britain from a pilgrimage, was disappointed in love and ended his days living as a hermit in a cave that he carved for himself by the river. That was in 929 and the place has borne his name ever since.

The Avon divides Warwick and Royal Leamington Spa, and the River Leam joins it on the border between the two towns which, but for this strand of water, would merge into one.

'Historic Warwick' boast the signs. It is no idle boast – Warwick drips with history. The jewel in the crown is Warwick Castle. Open every day except Christmas Day, it is described as 'the finest mediaeval castle in England'. It sits on a hill whence it commands

Marks on the masonry of Ashow Church are signs of earlier archery practice – arrows were sharpened here.

sensational views of the meandering river and countryside beyond.

Founded by Ethelfleda, daughter of Alfred the Great, in 915, the majority of the building seen today dates from the fourteenth century. It had a chequered history, passing through regal and noble hands – notably the Earls of Warwick – until, in 1978, it was sold to Madame Tussaud's. The company have left their mark by installing figures in some of the rooms so that you can attend a 'Royal Weekend Party, 1898' but it is done with taste. When you have toured the Castle, spare some time for the gardens and grounds and the handiwork of Lancelot 'Capability' Brown.

Between Stratford and Warwick is the richest area of the river in terms of wildlife. Disturbance of the river-bank habitats is kept to a minimum and plants, birds and animals enjoy the privacy. Stop for a last look on the eighteenth-century Castle Bridge that spans the river just south of the town. Then turn and head for Barford.

The river-crossing settlement of Stanlei, or Stoneleigh, remains largely unspoiled. The blacksmith still shoes horses on the village green.

There was once a water-mill here. I wish I didn't have to keep saying that. A free source of power, no longer utilised due to fluctuating water levels and abstraction; perhaps when we are gone, society will once more turn to this source of energy which combined the picturesque with the powerful.

In mediaeval times any swift-flowing river would be harnessed at frequent intervals to grind the grain to make the flour for bread. Gradient and

Guy's Cliffe is a spot named for Guy of Warwick who ended his days there in a cave, but the ruinous Guy's Cliffe House was a Georgian mansion built around 1751 for Samuel Greatheed. Sarah Siddons, the actress, was once a lady's maid here.

underlying soil would govern the depth and consistency of the water flow, which in turn governed the spacing of the mills. On less reliable water courses, such as those on chalk downs, mills would occasionally cease to work, and in a dry season a duck could bring off a brood before the wheel turned once more.

There were over six hundred water mills in the Warwick area at the time of the Domesday survey, and the rents payable varied according to the amount of flour produced. The mill at Stratford-upon-Avon, for instance, paid a rent of ten shillings and 1000 eels.

At a bend in the Avon where the River Dene joins its flow is Charlecote Park, once the home of the Lucy family and now a National Trust property.

The Clopton Bridge across the river at Stratford-upon-Avon was named after Hugh Clopton, a Stratford merchant who became Lord Mayor of London in 1492. Part of it was removed for improved defences during the Civil War.

Warwick Castle dates from 915, but visitors today can enjoy an Edwardian House Party courtesy of Madame Tussaud's. It's all in the best possible taste!

Through Alveston the Avon runs on to its most famous town, Stratford-upon-Avon, under the fourteen stone arches of Clopton Bridge, built in 1485 and named after Hugh Clopton, a Stratford merchant who became Lord Mayor of London in 1492. Part of the bridge was demolished during the Civil War to ensure the county's security.

The river was responsible for the founding of the town by Romano-British settlers. The river gravel ensured the foundations for their dwellings were well drained, the soils light and easily ploughed, and the water clean and pure.

William Shakespeare was baptised in Holy Trinity Church on the banks of the Avon on 26 April 1564, and died on 23 April 1616. The church contains a memorial to him, as well as the registers of his birth and burial. The town boasts his birthplace, the place where he died (New Place, which is now an Elizabethan garden), Hall's Croft (the home of his daughter Susanna), and at nearby Shottery on the edge of the town is the thatched cottage of his wife, Anne Hathaway.

Parts of the Old Town still have much charm, but there are other areas that have caught the contagious disease sweeping through many of Britain's old towns – that of plastic illuminated signs and modern pedestrian precincts.

The Royal Shakespeare Theatre sits right on the bank of the Avon. Built in 1932 to replace the previous structure which burned down in 1926, it was nicknamed the 'Jam Factory'.

Holy Trinity Church, Stratford-upon-Avon – Shakespeare was baptised and buried here.

Rowing boats glide by on the river, and a seat on the verandah of the theatre on a summer's day with a light lunch is a pleasure.

Tourists have come here for a long time, and often by way of the Avon. Navigation was improved between Evesham and Stratford in 1672 and boats as heavy as 30 tons could reach the mooring by the present Memorial Theatre. In the seventeenth century there were plans to make Stratford a great river port, but they came to nothing, even though coal barges did make their way up here.

Fishermen come here now. The Birmingham Anglers Association owns the rights and is one of the country's largest fishing clubs. Roach, chub, dace and perch can be found here and this is the furthest point upstream reached by barbel from the Severn.

Stratford is the upstream limit of navigation on the Avon though there are moves to extend the limit to Warwick, a prospect which does not appeal to conservationists who foresee much destruction of habitat if this should happen.

Time to move on. South of Stratford

the River Stour joins the Avon, bringing with it mineral deposits from the Cotswolds through which it has travelled. Past Luddington and Weston to the second Welford-on-Avon. There are new buildings in this village, but also plenty of old half-timbered and thatched properties, and a striped maypole on the village green.

The Avon Valley Footpath follows the river for a few miles now and above it on the way to Bidford-on-Avon is the reputedly haunted Hillborough – a grey gabled mansion.

Happier stories attach to Bidford-on-Avon. At the Falcon Inn (still standing, though now an antique shop) Shakespeare is reputed to have taken part in a drinking competition with his fellows from Stratford.

There has been a river-crossing here for centuries. In Roman times it was a ford, but today's eight-arched bridge was built in the fifteenth century. It struggles to cope with twentieth-century traffic, but narrow-boats are less troubled on the water.

At Cleeve Prior, whose Manor House has superbly clipped yews, the river flows out of Warwickshire and into Worcestershire. From the river, across Worcester Meadows, are Salford Priors and Abbots Salford, where the Elizabethan Salford Hall stands. Once a nunnery, it is now a hotel and restaurant. Harvington Mill, downstream, is derelict. Maybe I should just stop mentioning them.

But now we enter growing country – the Vale of Evesham – passing through Offenham which gave its name

Welford-on-Avon still boasts half-timbered thatched cottages and a maypole.

Club, too. You can fish for roach, chub, dace, perch and barbel, and for bream and pike below Evesham. There are river boat trips and the oldest rope-pulled ferry – the Hampton Ferry – operates in spring and summer, gently carrying its passengers across the waters in a punt-like craft.

With mediaeval buildings liberally sprinkled throughout the town, Evesham is still in touch with its past, even if it has come a long way since it was named after Eoves, swineherd to the Bishop of Worcester in the eighth century. It was Eoves who saw a vision of the Virgin Mary, which convinced Egwin, the Bishop, that a monastery should be founded here. Eoveshome, became Evesham, but the remains of the abbey are reminders of the early vision of a swineherd and the work of a bishop who became St Egwin.

to a cabbage, long after Offa, the King of Mercia, had given his name to the place itself. A ferry crosses the river here, to land walkers and fishermen on the opposite bank.

The market town of Evesham is at the heart of fruit-growing country. Come to the Vale of Evesham in blossom time and sigh. You can even follow a 'Blossom Trail' that is sign-posted from the High Street. Evesham Abbey, like so many others, was demolished at the Dissolution of the Monasteries, but the Lichfield Bell Tower, dating from 1533, remains.

The Evesham Rowing Club has been sculling on the Avon for over a hundred years, and there is a Sailing

Evesham, in fruit-growing country, owes its foundation to a swineherd.

The river does a 'U' turn in Evesham and heads north past the site of the Battle of Evesham when, in 1265, Simon de Montfort, Earl of Leicester was defeated by Prince Edward, son of Henry III.

This is now the lower Avon – the upper Avon being above the weir in Evesham. From here to Tewkesbury the water is easily navigable and there is much to-ing and fro-ing of pleasure craft, and opening and closing of locks.

Fladbury, where the river flows north-east of Evesham, is especially associated with the river's navigability, being the home of William Sandys who busied himself making the river suitable for traffic as far back as 1636.

There are more mills – Fladbury Mill and Cropthorne Mill (neither working) – before you come to Pershore, a Georgian town, once the site of a Benedictine Abbey. Part of the abbey serves as the parish church and the fourteenth-century lantern tower also survives.

There is also a fourteenth-century six-arched bridge over the Avon which leads to Pershore but a newer version has taken the weight off its back. This is a town that will forever be associated with plums. It is also a town whose

Hampton Ferry is said to be the oldest rope-pulled ferry. Hamptonians are hauled across the Avon by boat to shop in Evesham.

happiness will be governed by the state of the weather at blossom time; a late frost can be disastrous.

There are marsh warblers on the river here – one of Britain's rarest breeding birds. They are protected and their habitat preserved. Kingfishers crop up all along the river.

Now southwards flows the Avon, underneath Bredon Hill, in delightful countryside, speckled with unspoiled villages. Be tempted to climb the hill and gaze on the Cotswolds, over Pershore and towards Tewkesbury. On a clear day, they say you can see eight counties from here; some say fourteen.

Past Eckington and the oldest stone bridge on the now robust river, the waters of the Avon glide down an open vale past Strensham and Bredon. There is a smart sailing club at North Bredon Quay, and the tower of St Giles Church is a beauty at 161 feet.

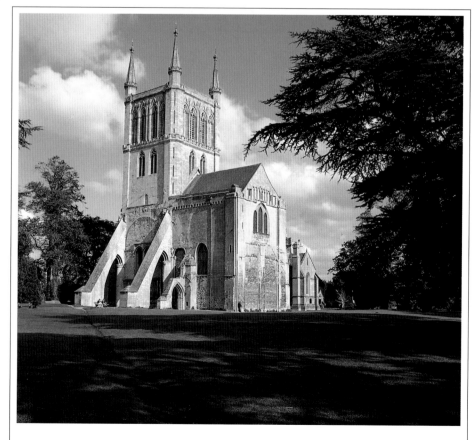

Pershore Abbey was founded around 972 and survived intact until the Dissolution in 1540. The choir, south transept and tower remain and are used as the parish church.

The M5 motorway comes too close to Bredon for comfort, and the river passes under it past Twyning to Tewkesbury. On the outskirts of the town the waters split – part of the river becomes the 'Old Avon' and travels through the Severn Ham pasture, and part of it becomes Mill Avon and flows through Tewkesbury town. There is a rarity in the waters here. The twaite shad, a relative of the herring, comes upriver as far as Tewkesbury to spawn.

Once the site of the Battle of Tewkesbury – one of the bloodiest battles in the Wars of the Roses in 1471 – Tewkesbury is today best known for its abbey which is 900 years old and the last of the monasteries to be dissolved by King Henry VIII. The townspeople bought the abbey from the King for £453 and it is now used as a parish church.

The last mill on the Avon, the Abbey Mill, or Abel Fletcher's Mill, ceased to dirty its hands for a living in the 1920s and has now become a restaurant. There has been a mill on this spot since 1200. It was renamed after the character who was said to own it in Mrs Craik's *John Halifax, Gentleman*, written in 1856. Although it now offers bread rather than flour to its patrons, it does still possess the machinery to grind the corn, which has been preserved rather like horse brasses on the wall of a country pub. The Avon, as if knowing it is no longer needed for hard work, passes through Tewkesbury, and at Lower Lode it joins the Severn for the journey to the Bristol Channel.

Abbey Mill, on the Avon at Tewkesbury, ceased grinding corn in the 1920s. There has been a mill here for 700 years.

At Tewkesbury, half-timbered houses occupy the Avon waterfront along with pleasure-craft which can cruise upstream to Stratford-upon-Avon.

The Cumbrian Derwent

Height at source: 1960 feet
Length: 33 miles
Runs from Seathwaite Fell to Workington

…the fairest of all rivers, loved
To blend his murmurs with my nurse's song.

The Prelude by William Wordsworth, 1805

The combined waters of several Cumbrian gills combine to make the Derwent a noisy, tumbling torrent in times of wet weather, and a gentle trickle in summer droughts. It is a river of fickle temperament.

High up on Seathwaite Fell in Cumbria, sandwiched between Great Gable and Scafell Pike, is Sprinkling Tarn, the moorland pool where the Derwent has its source. It is aptly named. The village of Seathwaite, below the fell, is the wettest inhabited place in Britain. Totals between 131 and 157 inches are quoted, but the Meteorological Office in Bracknell reckons the village had a drenching of 125 inches a year on average between 1961 and 1990 – about four times as much as most parts of the country.

The lakes are at their best in spring or early autumn – times when they are less peopled and the lighting softer. Perversely, holidaying near Seathwaite in summer a few years ago we enjoyed one of the driest and quietest weeks we have ever had. From our base there was a chance to climb Great Gable and Bow Fell with a dog in tow. (Until you have carried a labrador up the summit of Great Gable you haven't lived.)

In these parts, Wainwright's Fell Guides are indispensable. These are the Southern Fells, which include

On the fellside to the west of Seathwaite, Sour Milk Gill splashes and spills its way over rocks to join the Derwent in a spectacular waterfall.

England's highest peak, Scafell Pike at 3210 feet, so it is not surprising that of Seathwaite Fell the great man says:

...the fell itself, with few attractions to compare with those of the greater mountains around, is rarely visited – except, of course, by the custodian of the infamous rain gauges...

The fellside stream makes its way from Sprinkling Tarn (described by Lakeland artist W. Heaton Cooper as 'the most completely satisfying of all the tarns of Lakeland') to Styhead Tarn. Then, under the name of Styhead Gill,

it heads for Taylorgill Force where it hurtles over rocks before joining up with Grains Gill. At their union the two gills become the Derwent proper and tumble towards Seathwaite.

The village is not of any great size but there is a small fish farm at the aptly named Raingauge Farm. The water of the Derwent is of good quality for fish but there are occasional problems with acid rain. And it is not only fish which are susceptible to changes in acidity. Some lichens have a problem growing here now. Seathwaite is a

suitable starting point for walkers attempting either Great Gable or Scafell Pike, and it is to this end that most folk come here.

In spite of the fact that this is an area of high rainfall, the Derwent can dry up in summer. What is left of the flow makes its way underground, leaving shallow pools on the river bed.

The road accompanies the river northwards down the valley to Seatoller, a thriving community during the lead-mining days of the seventeenth and eighteenth centuries. Nowadays the only people carrying picks in these parts are rock climbers.

The steep-sided valley that runs from here down to Derwent Water is considered by many to be the most beautiful part of Lakeland. It is Borrowdale. The lower slopes of the five-mile-long valley are wooded, the hillsides carpeted with pasture and then the majestic Lakeland fells tower above. This is Herries country. Sir Hugh Walpole lived on the Brackenburn estate on the west side of the valley during the latter part of his life and wrote his *Herries Chronicle* here in the early 1930s.

Past Johnny Wood, an oak and sycamore wood so rich in mosses, ferns and liverworts that it has been designated a Site of Special Scientific Interest, through Rosthwaite with its stone cottages, the valley begins to narrow into the Jaws of Borrowdale.

The entrance to Borrowdale is towered over by Castle Crag on the west (the site of a fort erected by the Britons to repel the Romans) and has the famous Bowder Stone on the east. This 2000-ton granite boulder was deposited here by glacial activity. It perches perilously on one of its corners and twenty-nine steps will take you to its top. The view is one to treasure.

Herons glide over the river and its contributing gills, there are disused mines and quarries, and the famous green slate of this part of Lakeland is everywhere in evidence.

A handsome double-arched stone bridge crosses the river at Grange, whose cottages nestle below the fells around a small green. The village takes its name from the fact that it was an abbey farm and granary for the Cistercian monks of Furness Abbey in the thirteenth century. It is the Derwent's last port of call before it flows across pasture and reed beds into the lake known as Derwent Water.

For a panorama of the 'Queen of the Lakes', turn off the B5289 towards Watendlath and stop at Surprise View. There you will see the lake in all its glory – provided the mists allow. Behind it rises Cat Bells, an easy-to-climb fell that offers magical views and happy memories for Beatrix Potter readers. It was here that Mrs Tiggy-winkle distributed her washing.

Derwent Water has a wide range of liquid pleasures, aside from the foaming tankards of its hostelries.

Fisherman can find roach, ruffe, pike and trout within its waters, and salmon move through it on their way upstream. The waters of Watendlath

Derwent Water – 'The Queen of the Lakes' – with the slopes of Cat Bells rising behind it. It is a lake that is gazed at by walkers, satisfies fishermen, and has inspired writers through the centuries.

Beck tumble over boulders to make the Lodore Falls before entering the lake at its south-eastern corner, and above it you can find wagtails and dippers enjoying the strong current.

The Lakeland poet Robert Southey became poet laureate in 1813 but is chiefly remembered as the author of *The Three Bears*. He also wrote an onomatopoeic rhyme for his children, 'The Cataract of Lodore'. The 121 lines were based on a letter he wrote to his brother:

How does the Water come down at Lodore? ...rattling and battling, and shaking and quaking, and pouring and roaring, and waving and raving...

and so on. It became a party-piece for Victorian middle-class children. One can only presume Southey went there in very wet weather.

The road keeps to the eastern side of the lake but there are frequent temptations to depart from it – at Ashness Bridge, where a stone hump-backed bridge provides a photo-opportunity for tourists. At Friar's Crag there are more views across the lake, plus a monument to John Ruskin, writer and artist, who recalled:

The first thing I remember, as an event in life, was being taken by my nurse to the brow of Friar's Crag on Derwent Water; the intense joy, mingled with awe, that I had in looking through the hollows in the mossy roots, over the crag into the dark lake, has ever associated itself more or less with all twining roots of trees ever since.

Ruskin was not alone; many artists found inspiration in this part of the world, among them Constable, Gainsborough and Turner.

There are several islands on the lake and the largest of these is St Herbert's Island, home to St Herbert (a friend of St Cuthbert of Lindisfarne) from 685. As St Herbert died in 687 he must have had a short life of seclusion on the island. The ruins of a circular stone building are said to be the remains of his cell. The island, like Cat Bells, also features in Beatrix Potter. It is 'Owl Island', to which Squirrel Nutkin sails on his raft. Beatrix Potter wrote the story while staying at Lingholm on the western shores of the lake. Then, as now, it was the home of Lord Rochdale, and its gardens are open each year from April to October to show everything from spring bulbs and rhododendrons to specimen trees and shrubs – all set off by an amazing backdrop.

Of the other islands, Lord's Island was once home to the Earl of Derwentwater, and a group of German miners lived on Derwent Island in 1565. Joseph Pocklington, a banker, bought Derwent Island (or Vicar's Island as it then was) in 1778 and built a house and assorted follies upon it.

The village of Grange was once a farm and granary belonging to the monks of Furness Abbey. A stone bridge crosses the Derwent here.

The Lodore Falls – not always so turbulent as Robert Southey would have us believe for, like the Derwent, they are susceptible to drought.

The buzzard is resident in Cumbria, covering the hilly terrain with soaring leisurely sweeps and emitting its characteristic 'mewing' cry.

Only a nineteenth-century villa now remains and the island is in private hands.

Extravagant in his building tastes, Pocklington made his mark around here in the late eighteenth century, but Barrow Hall (the Youth Hostel) is the sole survivor. He also held regattas on the lake, and you can still get about on Derwent Water today.

There is a theatre here, and the Century Theatre group perform each summer by the launch car park. There is no waterskiing on Derwent Water, unlike Windermere, and there are restrictions on the launching of boats with outboard engines, which makes for a slightly quieter life. Brandelhow Park runs down to the western shore. In 1902 it became the first National Trust property in the Lake District.

At the north end of Derwent Water is Keswick which, to many folk, is the capital of the Lakes. Keswick today is a mine of information for the tourist but for around four hundred years it was a mine of industry.

Iron and copper were dug during the reign of Elizabeth I, and a shortage of labour meant that miners were brought over from Germany. (Some of them lived on Derwent Island, tending allotments and brewing beer.) When these mines were worked out, the extraction of graphite (then known as plumbago) continued through the eighteenth and early nineteenth centuries, bringing Keswick renown for the manufacture of pencils. The last graphite mine closed in 1838 but Keswick still produces pencils, importing its graphite from Sri Lanka, Korea, China and Russia. There is even a pencil museum.

The railway brought tourists here in the nineteenth century. Now it has gone and they come by car and coach. The town swarms with them in summer and even the Moot Hall (restored in the nineteenth century) has become an information centre. The River Greta surrounds it on three sides before joining up with the Derwent just north of the lake.

Greta Hall, now part of Keswick School, was lived in by both the poets Samuel Taylor Coleridge and Robert Southey. The town has a long association with poets. Shelley came here as a newly-wed, and Thomas Gray visited, as did the Wordsworths and Charles Lamb. Sir Hugh Walpole is buried in the south-west corner of St John's churchyard, within sight of the fells he so revered.

After Keswick, let the mighty slopes of Skiddaw tempt you northwards to follow the Derwent to Bassenthwaite Lake on the next leg of its journey to the Solway Firth.

Bassenthwaite is altogether quieter than Derwent Water and for me has pleasant memories of evening suppers at the Pheasant Inn on return journeys from the parish church choir trips of my youth. Within the waters of Bassenthwaite Lake are found vendace.

Ashness Bridge, near Derwent Water, is a much-loved spot for photographers; even the front of the Ordnance Survey map displays its simple beauty.

Southey is buried in Crosthwaite churchyard on the edge of the town. The church, dedicated to St Kentigern (known also as St Mungo), is the oldest building in Keswick.

Here and in Derwent Water is the only habitat for this whitefish, a survivor from the Ice Age which, at one time, could be found in Scottish lochs. Now the vendace is a protected species.

There is a theatre on the lakeside below Mirehouse, and at the north end of Bassenthwaite Lake the fell sides recede to give a gentler feeling to the landscape. Skiffs and dinghies quietly ply the waters.

The river leaves the top of the lake by flowing under Ouse Bridge – a three-arched nineteenth-century structure. On the gravel by the bridge, salmon spawn on their way upstream at the beginning of the year.

A few miles downstream the river turns south and meets the River Cocker at Cockermouth. This is a market town with a castle dating back to Norman times, though the majority of it dates from the fourteenth century. Cockermouth is not what you might call a pretty place but it does have one tourist attraction: the birthplace of William Wordsworth. The eighteenth-century house, with its porticoed doorway, saw the arrival of its famous son in 1770. His father was agent to the Earl of Lonsdale and the house

went with the job. Now it is owned by the National Trust and has, as estate agents put it, 'many original features'.

Swollen with the waters of the River Cocker, the Derwent now heads westwards to the sea, through lush dairy farming country and past the spoil heaps of now disused coal mines. For twenty years or more open-cast mining has taken their place.

The river flows past Brigham, at whose church Wordsworth's son John was a minister for forty years. It then proceeds to Great Clifton and Seaton

and on to the port of Workington.

Once there was a Roman fort here but it is for industry that Workington is best known today, and for iron and coal retrieved from the sea. Bessemer pioneered steel-making in the town and the prevailing smell now is of industrial processes, rather than the moorland heather that the Derwent passes over at its source.

The river reaches the end of its journey where Mary Queen of Scots started her long exile. It was to Workington Old Hall, now a sad ruin,

There are round trips on Derwent Water from Keswick, and smaller craft can be hired to explore.

The Cumbrian Derwent

The Church of St Bega sits beside Bassenthwaite Lake near Mirehouse.

Farmland and woodland run alongside Bassenthwaite Lake. The lake itself, and much of the woodland, is designated a Site of Special Scientific Interest.

that she came as a guest of the Curwen family, and from here that she wrote her letter of appeal to Elizabeth I: 'I entreat you to send for me as soon as possible, for I am in a pitiable condition, not only for a queen, but even for a gentlewoman.'

Elizabeth did not send for her and Mary perished on the block nineteen years later. The Derwent has a more productive end to its life, being used in the manufacture of steel, chemicals and paper. At Yearl Weir the National Rivers Authority has a fish counter which has recorded as many as six hundred salmon and sea trout moving upriver in one night, and porpoises have been spotted in the estuary.

Moves are underway to make this oligotrophic river (low in nutrients but rich in oxygen) an SSSI for the whole of its length, to protect the nutrient balance and so safeguard the sensitive wildlife within its waters. With any luck, and if there is any justice, it will happen.

The waters of the Cumbrian Derwent run into the sea at Workington. Lakeland is but a memory.

Index

Page numbers in *italic* refer to illustrations